A Preface to Auden

Allan Rodway

Longman   London and New York

LONGMAN GROUP LIMITED
Longman House,
Burnt Mill, Harlow, Essex, CM20 2JE, England
and Associated Companies throughout the World

Published in the United States of America
by Longman Inc. New York.

First published 1984

Library of Congress Cataloging in Publication Data

Rodway, Allan Edwin.
  A preface to Auden.
  (Preface books)
  Bibliography: p. 163
  Includes index.
  1. Auden, W. H. (Wystan Hugh), 1907–1973 –
Criticism and interpretation. I. Title.
PR6001.U4Z79   811'.52   82–6571
ISBN 0-582-35325-4   AACR2
ISBN 0-582-35326-2 (pbk.)

Set in 10/11 Baskerville, Monophoto

Printed in Hong Kong by
Wing King Tong Co. Ltd.

Dr Allan Rodway is Reader in English at the University of Nottingham. He
has written considerable material upon the Romantic period, upon the nature
of comedy and on the concepts underlying modern literary criticism and its
study in universities. He has published a volume of poetry and his most recent
publication is *The Craft of Criticism*, Cambridge University Press, 1982.

Contents

List of illustrations

Foreword

W. H. Auden, fittingly the first subject of a volume in the series of Preface Books to be born in our own century, stands therefore possibly too close to our own social indecisions and individual preoccupations for a consensus of critical opinion to have hardened over his work. Is it, we may ask, the English Auden, capable in the words of his contemporary Geoffrey Grigson of 'raising ordinary speech into strong or strange incantation', or the American poet of the same name adding his personal variety of Protestantism to an equally distinct use of the insights of psychology that is likely to dominate in future literary histories? Allan Rodway encourages the reader to ponder and reiterate many issues for himself by providing a comprehensive treatment of his subject, sketching several different contexts among the arts, sciences and opinions of Auden's day and not, as in a thesis, forcing us to reach his subject in only one way.

Dr Rodway's particular critical skill, as a poet himself, emerges in the close critical attention he pays to a small group of Auden's poems chosen from both the English and the American periods. Here every reader will profit from the careful demonstration of Auden's command of tone and idiom and the massive articulation of language that is everywhere apparent. From these analyses it is manifest that Auden justified throughout his career the position he quickly attained as the leader of a. generation that followed Yeats and Eliot. Among the most valuable parts of the book for me is the study of the poem 'The Shield of Achilles', significantly one of the productions of the later part of Auden's career.

As appreciation of the poet's work grows Allan Rodway shows why it has done so, for Auden is well understood as a man of great breadth and individuality and full of comments on living in the mid-twentieth century that have become not only essential material for our anthologies but have also provided the source of seven columns of entries in *The Oxford Dictionary of Quotations*.

MAURICE HUSSEY
General Editor

Introduction

This book conforms to the established pattern of the 'Preface' series, in that it surrounds the centrepiece – the critical assessment of the author's creative work – with a good deal of background information: cultural, political, biographical, and geographical. Most critical interpretation requires such peripheral support, to some degree, if the author's words on the page are to be fully understood. This procedure, however, is accompanied by two dangers: the danger of reading them so much by the light of background illumination that we see meanings that are not really there, because we expect them to be there, and the danger of reading poems as cultural or biographical documents while imagining they are being read as literature. Moreover, some authors require less by way of background (or some kinds of background) than others do. Thus, though we need to know something of the Elizabethan period in order to understand Shakespeare's work properly, the fact that we know next to nothing of his private life has probably been positively beneficial. Auden's is a similar case.

Just as Shakespeare disappears behind his characters, so Auden tends to disappear behind his subjects and themes – and indeed, often, behind a dramatic persona adopted to express and explore them. So the political and cultural contexts of his poetry are usually much more relevant than any biographical or geographical context; for his poems are more often rooted in the ideas and events of his times than in the details of his life and personality. Auden is not a romantic, intent on expressing *himself*; he is intent on expressing a subject, a theme, on exploring an idea of a common human predicament, or on placing his own feelings objectively. Like the hawk and the airman that make symbolic appearances in his poetry, he sees things impersonally and in a long perspective. Even his love-poetry meditates rather than emotes.

He himself was strongly opposed both to the egotism of self-expression and to biographical studies of authors – a disapproval reinforced in the latter case by requests to friends to destroy his letters. It comes as no surprise to find him quoting with strong approval a letter of Housman's about a would-be interviewer:

> Tell him that the wish to include a glimpse of my personality in a literary article is low, unworthy, and American. Tell him that some men are more interesting than their books but my book is more interesting that its man ... Tell him anything else that you think will put him off.
>
> (*Forewords and Afterwords*, ed. Mendelson, p. 325)*

*Throughout the text, as here, somewhat abbreviated references are given. For full references, see Bibliography, p. 163.

In justification of this attitude we may cite not only Auden's habit of adopting different personae (a cause of difficulty in poems that is removable only by *literary* interpretation), but also the many poems in which too close attention to biographical or geographical matters would be positively misleading. It is often said, for instance, of one of his most renowned poems 'In Praise of Limestone' that it derives from Auden's memories of the limestone landscape of the Yorkshire dales that he knew in his early years. Well, perhaps it did *derive* from them. But at best that would explain only how the poem came about; it would not explain what it finally came to be. Indeed, it might well cause the geographically fixated reader to miss the fact, or at any rate the implications of the fact, that this landscape features hilltop temples, vineyards, and fountains – characteristic of classical Greece or Italy but hardly of the Yorkshire dales. For, whatever it started from, this has become a *compound* landscape, a *type* of landscape that might be found anywhere anytime; and it is contrasted with other typical landscapes and their symbolically generalised inhabitants. Again, when Auden writes of 'the City' it is not Birmingham, London, or New York – the cities he lived in – that are relevant to his meaning. It is *any* city; it is the idea of the city: the city as contrasted with 'the country' – or even with 'islands', by which time 'the City' has come to symbolise the claims and obligations of civilised society as against the secluded personal life.

It is therefore particularly important in Auden's case not to be misled into reading what his poems might be supposed to say, in the light of extrinsic knowledge, instead of what they actually do say; not to imagine, for example, a Yorkshire dale or New York instead of a hypothetical landscape or townscape. Nevertheless, if this caution is borne in mind, the background may prove fairly helpful; for indications of why a poem or passage came about often help to elucidate just what it is that has come about, and knowledge of particular events or fields of thought (such as the Slump, the Spanish Civil War, or Marxism, Freudianism, and Existentialism in Auden's case) may clarify a poem that takes them for granted rather than referring to them specifically – though even then one has to bear in mind that Auden never swallowed any doctrine whole or merely versified an orthodoxy. More of his difficulties, too, are of a literary, than an ideological nature.

For these reasons the critical section of this book is more substantial than the background sections. In general, quotations are taken from Mendelson's *Collected Poems*, which gives Auden's final, revised versions. Where the revised version is significantly (rather than merely technically) different from the original version, Mendelson's *The English Auden* has always been preferred. The poems given *detailed* critical treatment, in Part Two, are all to be found in Mendelson's *Selected Poems*, which prints the Thirties' poetry in the original versions.

Part One:

The Poet and His Setting

Chronological table 1

AUDEN'S LIFE　　　　　　SELECTED POLITICAL EVENTS

1907　Wystan Hugh Auden born
　　　at York (21 February), third
　　　son of George and
　　　Constance

1908　Removal to Birmingham,
　　　where George Auden took
　　　up posts of School Medical
　　　Officer for the city and
　　　Professor of Public Health at
　　　the University

1910　　　　　　　　　　　　　　　Death of Edward VII

1915　Boarder at St Edmund's　　First World War
−20　　School, Hindhead, Surrey,
　　　where he meets
　　　Christopher Isherwood

1916　　　　　　　　　　　　　　　Irish Rebellion defeated

1917　　　　　　　　　　　　　　　The Russian Revolution

1920　Enters Gresham's School,
　　　Holt, Norfolk, becoming star
　　　pupil

1922　Ceases to believe in religion,　Home Rule for Southern
　　　publishes first poem, 'Dawn',　Ireland (followed by Civil
　　　in school magazine　　　　　War)

1922　　　　　　　　　　　　　　　Fascist rule in Italy, under
−45　　　　　　　　　　　　　　　dictatorship of Mussolini

1924　　　　　　　　　　　　　　　(January) First Labour
　　　　　　　　　　　　　　　　Government, led by Ramsay
　　　　　　　　　　　　　　　　MacDonald; by November
　　　　　　　　　　　　　　　　Conservatives, under
　　　　　　　　　　　　　　　　Baldwin, were in power

2

1925	Goes up to Christ Church, Oxford, as exhibitioner in Natural Sciences; briefly switches to P.P.E. (Politics, Philosophy and Economics); finally takes English, having Nevill Coghill as tutor Brilliant, but inexplicably gets a third-class degree	
1926		The General Strike
1928	Goes to Berlin, learns German – a language he later perfected himself in	
1929	Tutors in London	Beginnings of Depression in the U.S.A.
1930		Beginnings of the Slump in U.K.
1930 –32	Schoolmaster at Larchfield Academy, Helensburg, Scotland	
1931		Britain goes off Gold Standard 'Coalition' Government takes over until 1937 Japan invades Manchuria
1932		British Union of Fascists founded by Sir Oswald Mosley
1932 –35	Schoolmaster at Downs School, Colwell, Northumberland	
1933		Nazis, led by Hitler, come to power in Germany Germany leaves League of Nations Italy invades Abyssinia Baldwin succeeds MacDonald

1935	Marries Erika Mann (daughter of Thomas Mann) to provide her with a British passport in order to assist her escape from Germany Begins six months with G.P.O. film unit as writer and assistant director	
1936	Visits Iceland with Louis MacNeice	Hitler invades the Rhineland General Franco's troops rebel against the Spanish Government Death of George V Abdication of Edward VIII Spanish Civil War 1936–39
1937	Visits Spain, broadcasts for the Republican government Teaches at Downs School again	Baldwin and MacDonald retire Conservative Government under Chamberlain, till May 1940, when 'national' government is formed with Winston Churchill as P.M.
1938	Travels to China with Christopher Isherwood and, returning via Japan and U.S.A., takes decision to live in America	Hitler invades Austria (March) The Munich Agreement Chamberlain offers the Sudeten lands of Czechoslavakia to Hitler (September)
1939	Departs for New York Lives in Brooklyn Heights till 1941 Meets Chester Kallman, with whom he shared most of the rest of his life and collaborated on a number of opera libretti	Czechoslavakia partitioned between Germany and Hungary Nazi-Soviet pact Russia invades Poland and Finland Hitler invades Poland (31 August) Second World War 1939–45

1940	Begins a year's teaching at New School for Social Research, New York Reconverted to Christianity, takes Anglican communion	Fall of France Italy declares war
1941	Teaches at writers' conference at Olivet College, Michigan Begins year's teaching at Michigan University	U.S.S.R., Japan and U.S.A. enter war
1942	Begins three years' teaching at Swarthmore College; in the latter two also teaching at Bryn Mawr College	Montgomery defeats Rommel at Alamein
1945	With the U.S. forces in Europe, as a civilian research officer (ranking as major) in Morale Division of U.S. Strategic Bombing Survey Visits England for first time since 1939 Moves to New York, living in various apartments	The destruction of Dresden by conventional bombing; destruction of Hiroshima and Nagasaki by atomic bombing Unconditional surrender of Germany and Japan United Nations Organisation Charter UNESCO First Labour Government with a majority in the House, under Attlee
1946	Teaches at Bennington College Becomes a naturalised American Begins one year's teaching at New School for Social Research	
1947	Teaches Religion at Barnard College	

1948	Visits Ischia in Italy, renting a house there for spring and summer of every year from 1949 till 1957 Teaches at the New School for Social Research	
1950	Visiting lecturer at Mount Holyoke College	NATO Korean War (first U.N. resistance to aggression)
1951		E.E.C. inaugurated
1952		Birth control pill First H-bomb
1953	Settles at 77 St Mark's Place, New York till 1972 Research Professor at Smith College	
1956	Elected Professor of Poetry at Oxford for 5 years – a post requiring delivery of three public lectures *per annum*	England, France and Israel unsuccessfully attack Egypt, after nationalisation of Suez Canal Hungarian Revolution (crushed by USSR) *Sputnik I*
1958	Moves to a converted farmhouse in Kirchstetten, Lower Austria, where he spends each spring and summer for rest of his life	Castro becomes Premier of Cuba
1962		Kennedy elected U.S. President
1963		Kennedy assassinated
1964	Second visit to Iceland Begins six months in Berlin, as member of artists-in-residence programme sponsored by the Ford Foundation	Vietnam War India-Pakistan War

1968		Student unrest begins in Paris and spreads U.S.S.R. invades Czechoslovakia
1969		First Moon landing
1972	Returns to Oxford to live in cottage in grounds of Christ Church College	
1973	Dies during a weekend spent in Vienna on way back to Oxford from Kirchstetten Buried in churchyard at Kirchstetten	Britain joins Common Market U.S. withdraw from Vietnam Watergate scandal Arab-Israeli Yom Kippur War Oil Crisis

Chronological table 2

(excluding works edited, but not written by W. H. Auden)

AUDEN'S WORKS	SELECTED LITERARY EVENTS
1922	T. S. Eliot, *Waste Land* James Joyce, *Ulysses* D. H. Lawrence, *Fantasia of the Unconscious* Translations of Freud's *Interpretation of Dreams* and *Beyond the Pleasure Principle* and of Jung's *Psychological Types*
1928 *Poems*, privately printed by Stephen Spender in edition of about 45 copies	Bertolt Brecht, *The Threepenny Opera* C. Day Lewis, *Country Comets*
1930 *Poems* published by Faber & Faber, who remained Auden's English publishers till his death in 1973: the volume contained 30 poems and 'Paid on Both Sides' (2nd edition, replacing 7 poems, 1933)	Empson, *Seven Types of Ambiguity* Franz Kafka, *The Castle* C. Day Lewis, *From Feathers to Iron*
1932 *The Orators* (2nd edition 1934; 3rd edition 1966)	Christopher Isherwood, *The Memorial* 'McDiarmid', *First Hymn to Lenin* F. R. Leavis (ed.) *Scrutiny* – till 1953
1933 *The Dance of Death* published; produced by the Group Theatre, 25 February 1934	C. Day Lewis, *The Magnetic Mountain* David Gascoyne, *Man's Life is this Meat* Stephen Spender, *Poems*

1934	American edition of *Poems* (including *The Orators* and *The Dance of Death*)	
1935	*The Dog Beneath the Skin* (with Isherwood) published; produced by Group Theatre, 12 January 1936 *The Ascent of F6* (with Isherwood) published; produced by Group Theatre, 26 February 1937	C. Day Lewis, *A Time to Dance* Christopher Isherwood, *Mr Norris Changes Trains* and *Lions and Shadows* Louis MacNeice, *Poems* *The Faber Book of Modern Verse* (ed. Roberts)
1936	*Look Stranger!* The title was given by Faber's while Auden was in Iceland; he disliked it and titled the American edition (1937) *On This Island*	
1937	*Spain* – the royalties went to Medical Aid for Spain *Letters from Iceland* (with MacNeice)	George Barker, *Calamiterror* Wyndham Lewis, *The Revenge for Love* Franz Kafka, *The Trial*
1938	*On the Frontier* (with Isherwood) published; produced by Group Theatre, 14 November	C. Day Lewis, *Overtures to Death*
1939	*Education Today and Tomorrow* (pamphlet, with T. C. Worsley) *Journey to a War* (with Isherwood) published	T. S. Eliot, *The Family Reunion* and *The Idea of a Christian Society* Christopher Isherwood, *Goodbye to Berlin* Louis MacNeice, *Autumn Journal* Stephen Spender, *The Still Centre*
1940	*Another Time*	George Barker, *Lament and Triumph* C. Day Lewis, *Poems in Wartime*

1941	*The Double Man* (English title: *New Year Letter*) *Paul Bunyan* (operetta to music by Britten) performed at Columbia University	Louis MacNeice, *Plant and Phantom*
1942		Thornton Wilder, *The Skin of our Teeth* C. Day Lewis, *Word Over All*
1944	*For the Time Being* (including 'The Sea and The Mirror')	T. S. Eliot, *Four Quartets* Louis MacNeice, *Springboard*
1945	*The Collected Poetry* (Auden disapproved of the title)	Christopher Isherwood, *Prater Violet* George Orwell, *Animal Farm*
1946		Louis MacNeice, *The Dark Tower* Stephen Spender, *Poems of Dedication*
1947	*The Age of Anxiety*	
1949		George Orwell, *1984* Christopher Isherwood, *The Condor and the Cows*
1950	*Collected Shorter Poems 1930–44* (British version of the 1945 edition) *The Enchafèd Flood* (prose)	George Barker, *The Dead Seagull* and *The True Confessions of George Barker*
1951	*Nones* *The Rake's Progress* (libretto with Kallman, music by Stravinsky) produced in Venice	
1954		Samuel Beckett, *Waiting for Godot* Dylan Thomas, *Under Milk Wood*

1955	*The Shield of Achilles*	Philip Larkin, *The Less Deceived* J. R. R. Tolkien, *The Lord of the Rings*
1956	*Making, Knowing and Judging* (pamphlet based on his inaugural lecture at Oxford)	John Osborne, *Look Back in Anger* William Golding, *Lord of the Flies* Ted Hughes, *The Hawk in the Rain*
1960	*Homage to Clio*	Harold Pinter, *The Caretaker*
1961	*Elegy for Young Lovers* (libretto with Kallman, music by Hans Werner Henze) performed at Stuttgart	Joseph Heller, *Catch 22*
1962	*The Dyer's Hand* (prose)	
1965	*About the House*	
1966	*The Bassarids* (libretto with Kallman, music by Henze) performed at Salzburg *Collected Shorter Poems 1925–57*	
1967		Tom Stoppard, *Rosencrantz and Guildenstern Are Dead* Ted Hughes, *Wodwo*
1968	*Collected Longer Poems* *Secondary Worlds* published (T. S. Eliot memorial lectures at University of Kent)	
1969	*City Without Walls*	
1970	*A Certain World* (a commonplace book)	John Fowles, *The French Lieutenant's Woman*

1971	*Academic Graffiti*	
1972	*Epistle to a Godson*	Tom Stoppard, *Jumpers*
1973	*Love's Labour's Lost* (libretto with Kallman, music by Nicholas Nabokov) performed in Brussels *Forewords and Afterwords* (prose)	
1974	*Thank You Fog* published posthumously	

1   Auden's Life

General

Though Wystan Hugh Auden, aptly nicknamed Uncle Wiz – committed himself, first, to a rather extreme political creed and, later, to a rather extreme religious one, little sense of emotional belief comes over; the commitment seems rather to be to a set of ideas; nor, in either case, does it seem to be an unqualified commitment. Similarly, though he was so individualistic as to count as an eccentric, little sense of a special personality comes through; one senses rather an independent intelligence curiously scanning various areas, testing for truth or, sometimes, seeking for stimulus. And what applies to politics and religion applies also to nature and art. Auden was far from unresponsive to aesthetic qualities but what he was primarily interested in was significances. When he says that the Old Masters were never wrong, in his 'Musée des Beaux Arts', for instance, it soon appears that he does not mean that they always got their composition and colouring right but that they were never wrong in their *ideas*. Perhaps it is not irrelevant that though he read English at Oxford he went up on a scholarship in natural sciences, and retained an interest in science throughout his life. Were the intelligence not as compassionate as it is ironic, it would be tempting to describe him paradoxically as a 'poetic scientist'.

That description will not quite do, but Auden does indeed seem at first sight incredibly paradoxical both in his life and his work. Not only was he first an atheistic Freudian communist and then a Christian, existentialist liberal, but also, first and last, he was metaphysical and materialistic, compassionate and clinical, orderly and untidy, generous and mean, brilliant and foolish, unhappy and optimistic, innovatory and traditionalist, joky and serious. Gradually, however, an underlying unity emerges. Thus both the communism and the Christianity are seen to spring from a common source: the wish to improve the world and its inhabitants. He always wished to be a redeemer of the wretched, though first as a sort of mountebank doctor, later as a sort of mountebank preacher – a cool-gospeller though, rather than a hot-gospeller. Cool analysis and a notable absence of self-deception are constantly characteristic. As early as 1933, for example, he is writing a love-poem so maturely clear-eyed as to be almost cynical:

> It is an enemy that sighs for you:
> Love has one wish and that is not to be.

Had you never been beautiful nor true
He would not have been born and I were free
From one whose whispers shall go on and on
Till you are false and all your beauties gone
            (*The English Auden*, ed. Mendelson, p. 147)

Always, too, there is sympathetic but not empathetic understanding, feeling-for rather than feeling-in: a product of his tendency to stand back, take a long view, place in perspective, perceive significantly, as in these lines from *Journey to a War*:

They are and suffer; that is all they do:
A bandage hides the place where each is living,
His knowledge of the world restricted to
The treatment that the instruments are giving
        ... We stand elsewhere.
For who when healthy can become a foot?
        ... Only happiness is shared,
And anger, and the idea of love.

                        (Ibid. p. 258)

Whether the underlying unity is quite the same in the poetry and the life is doubtful – or at any rate, whether it is always the same. Auden himself certainly believed that art and life were different and should not be confused. In principle and practice he was opposed to autobiographical poetry, save of the most factual kind (as in the light verse of his 'Letter to Lord Byron'). So his poems contain no revelations about his schooldays, his parents, his sex life, or his friendships. On the other hand, they do reflect the range of his intellectual interests and his constant tendency to try to see the general in the particular, the skeleton of articulated principles within the dense complicated body of practical life; his poems share, that is to say, the clinical and expository attitude he affected from his undergraduate youth, when he tutored his tutor, to the conversational punditry of his eminent old age; throughout, his manner was diagnostic and anti-romantic:

If Eliot sometimes seems a sidesman in a surplice, suspecting heresies, Auden's natural, and perhaps inherited, attitude is that of a clinician in a white coat, expecting epidemics of madness and hypochondria, the slow poisons that affect the whole political body and are natural disturbances of the mind.
            (Stuart Hampshire, 'A look back at the Collected Poems',
                    in *W. H. Auden: A Tribute**, ed. Spender, p. 224)

*This book, Charles Osborne's *W. H. Auden*, and Auden's *Letter to Lord Byron* are prime sources of biographical information. This section is indebted to all of them.

What Hampshire might have added was that it would certainly have been a *dirty* white coat. For Auden deprecated excessive cleanliness as a symptom of neurosis, and thought it unnecessary to have more than one suit – an indifference to appearance perhaps reinforced by that streak of meanness that kept strict surveillance over the supplies of toilet paper, and contrasted so strongly with his generosity to those in need. His indifference to appearance was such that he was sometimes taken for a tramp – once indeed when he had turned up to donate money to a charity for down-and-outs. The appalling untidiness of his rooms seems to have been an extension of this indifference: and is in startling contrast not only to his businesslike handling of money matters and his strictness with himself, guests, and lodgers about timekeeping, but also to the orderliness of his ideas, his regular working hours, his obsession with poetic craftsmanship and his admiration for the formal neatness and clarity of Pope, his favourite poet, and the civilised urbanity of Goethe and Horace. His own view was that untidiness and indifference in unimportant matters allowed more attention to be given to clarity and care in the important ones.

Certain of the eccentricities of this paradoxical poet – a sort of compassionate vivisectionist – individualistic and detached yet liking to *belong*, whether to a group or a Church, can be related to the apparently inconsistent qualities of his poetry or intellectual life. In general, of course, a habit of curious intellectualism, a readiness to try on different hats to see how they look and feel, an openness to speculation and rumination, must result in surface inconsistency – the underlying unity being provided precisely by that constant habit which gives such a result. Specific characteristics, however, of the life and the works sometimes do not seem to fit, or can be made to fit only with some strain to plausibility. Thus, though it *is* rational, in a way, to wear carpet slippers if you have bunions, few people would wear them, or could get away with wearing them, on all occasions: in the street, at formal functions, and even in the U.S. army, with his major's uniform, as Auden did; and rationality seems to disappear altogether when it comes to wearing *odd* slippers from differently coloured pairs. On the other hand, the trying-on of different personalities or different sets of ideas, to see what effect they had on himself or others, squares well enough with his habit of writing exploratory poetry, and of adopting different personae as the 'voices' for many poems. Even the habit of wolfing down his food (so fast that there are reports of his having finished sometimes before others at the same table had even been served) may fit in psychologically with his habit of voracious reading. His own account was that he hadn't time to waste over meals. Possibly, his lifelong custom of working all day with the curtains drawn and the light on, might be associated with the meditative, probing mode of his poetry, a poetry relying on insight rather than sight. However, it is difficult to resist applying the same sort of Freudian speculation to this

15

custom as Auden himself frequently indulged in. For he also liked to sleep under a heavy weight, and constantly amazed his hosts by taking down curtains and even framed pictures, or pulling up the stair carpet, to pile on his bed. Together with the close, dark room, this surely suggests a hidden death-wish, a secret longing for grave, tomb, or womb? If so, the relationship with his poetry in this case is an oblique one, in so far as the death-wish he attributed to the bourgeoisie in his Thirties' poetry could be a generalised projection of an unconscious death-wish of his own. Why ever, though, a tall man like Auden should have customarily sat on a volume of the *Oxford English Dictionary* 'as if he were a child too short for table' (Orlan Fox, 'Friday Nights', in *W. H. Auden: A Tribute*, ed. Spender) is beyond guessing. A poor and protracted joke on 'a seat of learning'? Or a substitute for a rostrum from which he could address the company?

Auden himself was well aware of his tendency to eccentricity and inconsistency, and played up to it in his youth. Later he reconciled it with his contra-tendency to strive for unity, coherence and system in two ways. Firstly, he felt that unity by exclusion was a cheat, a worthwhile coherence being one that involved the union of disparates; and secondly:

> [he] constantly maintained an inward debate that led him to answer a public exhortation like 'Spain' with the hermetic mysteries of a poem like 'Orpheus', written at about the same moment.
>
> (*Selected Poems*, ed. Mendelson, p. xiii)

Nor is eccentricity altogether out of keeping with the firm belief in individuality that made him so unconventional a communist and Christian – or, for that matter, with the rational belief that perfect conditioning would stifle originality:

> I hate the modern trick, to tell the truth,
>   Of straightening out the kinks in the young mind,
> Our passion for the tender plant of youth,
>   Our hatred for all weeds of every kind.
>   Slogans are bad: the best that I can find
> Is this: 'Let each child have that's in our care
> As much neurosis as the child can bear.'
>
> ('Letter to Lord Byron', *The English Auden*,
>   ed. Mendelson, p. 193)

These beliefs are directly relatable to the poetry as well as the life, to its immense variety of form, content, and mode:

> By all means let us touch our caps to
>   La Poésie pure, the epic narrative;
> But comedy shall get its round of claps too,
>   According to his power each may give;

Only on varied diet can we live.
The pious fable and the dirty story
Share in the total literary glory.

(Op.cit. p. 183)

This approval of comedy – a rather neglected aspect of Auden's work – goes with his humorous and self-critical temperament: qualities exemplified, for instance, in the stanzas of the 'Letter to Lord Byron' that conclude:

I have no proper eyebrows, and my eyes
Are far too close together to look nice.

(Op.cit. p. 189)

Or in his remark to Ursula Niebuhr:

We who profess ourselves Christians must not be allowed to forget how much justice there is in Nietzsche's assertion that as a whole we are a nastier lot than the pagans.

(*W. H. Auden: A Tribute*, ed. Spender, p. 117)

We can reconcile, too, Auden's lifelong interest in ancient myth on the one hand and modern machinery on the other: he works machines into modern myths. What seems impossible to reconcile, however, is the mellow maturity, the ease and wisdom and muted humour of the late poetry with the immense sadness, almost degradation that afflicted the man during his last years. Here, surely, it is right to respect Auden's view that poets are to be valued not for what they are but for how they write.

The Early Years

Born at York on the 21st February 1907, christened Wystan Hugh, Auden was the third son of his parents George and Constance – 'the lucky third son' of the fairy-tales and legends that enter into his poetry either explicitly or implicitly. Both parents were High Church Anglicans, but his father, as might be expected of a doctor with scientific interests, was a good deal less devout than his mother. In 1908 the family removed to Birmingham where George had obtained the posts of Schools Medical Officer for the city and Professor of Public Health at the University.

Birmingham, of course, gives easy access to the Yorkshire dales, and limestone landscapes became one of Auden's two favourite environments – the other being 'tramlines and slagheaps, pieces of machinery', gasworks and derelict canals. Even the limestone countryside was not of interest in its own right, as for a romantic, but only as an environment for man. He was at least as much interested in the lead mines as in the hills, in the bridges as the rivers.

From the beginning he was short-sighted, gifted, and precocious. The short-sightedness debarred him from proficiency at games, and probably further encouraged the voracious reading prompted by an inherently brilliant intelligence. It may also have furthered his early interest in music – though always music with words – which later resulted in his opera libretti. The bulk of his childish reading consisted of fairy-tales, myths and legends, especially Scandinavian ones, which he felt to be in keeping with the Norse origins of 'Auden' and the Saxon ones of 'Wystan' (an early saint), but this reading seems to have been almost matched by that of technical works on engineering, especially mining engineering; and he dismayed his aunts by talking, when a small child, like a professor of engineering. Psychology, too, was an early interest. At the age of eight he arrived confidently at his prep school, St Edmund's, Hindhead, announcing that he looked forward to studying the different types of boy. A highly significant approach to learning.

For four vital years of his childhood, of course, his father was absent on war service. This made him particularly close to his mother. His brother John has stated that Wystan never did escape from his mother (a fact that may well account for some of the oddities of his verse-drama *The Ascent of F6*); he has also stated that Wystan told him that the primary reason for his sudden conversion to religion was not, as Golo Mann suggested, a reading of Reinhold Niebuhr's *The Nature and Destiny of Man*, but the shock of his mother's death. Certainly that closeness at an impressionable age, and ten years in all-male boarding schools, may well explain the homosexuality that Auden early acknowledged in himself, never seems to have been disturbed by (at any rate on the surface), and never abandoned. Its influence on his work, were it not known of, would be literarily imperceptible; known, it is negligible.

At St Edmund's, Auden seems to have performed brilliantly without ever needing to try. He arrived two years later, and two years younger, than Christopher Isherwood – himself a very bright boy – but had caught him up by the fourth form. One mistress, Rosanina Bulley, recalls that he got the form prize and also first prize for mathematics. In 1920, he entered Gresham's School, Holt, where he became a star pupil. Still imbued with the ambition to be a mining engineer, he obtained an exhibition in natural science to Christ Church, Oxford. However, he soon switched to P.P.E. (politics, philosophy and economics) briefly, and then finally to English. The switch is not in fact as surprising as it might seem. He had started writing poetry at the age of fifteen, at the suggestion of a school friend, and had written a great deal before going up to Oxford. Between the ages of six and

Dr and Mrs Auden and their sons: (l. to r.) Wystan, Bernard and John

twelve, too, he had imagined in great detail a secret world. Its basic elements were limestone landscape and lead mines, its climate northern and autumnal. This favourite weather and scenery is often reflected in his verse, either directly or in the coolness and cragginess of its form. Nor was the brief flirtation with P.P.E. entirely out of keeping. Sir John Betjeman, an Oxford contemporary, recalls that Auden impressed him as a 'new type of undergraduate':

> I was the old type, trivial, baroque, incense-loving; a diner with great admiration for the landowning classes and the houses and parks in which they were lucky enough to live. Wystan was already aware of slum conditions in Birmingham and mining towns and docks. But he combined with this an intense interest in the geology and natural history and topography of the British isles.
>
> ('Oxford' in *W. H. Auden: A Tribute*, ed. Spender, p. 44)

The social awareness was to come to the fore in the interest in communism that Auden shared with Stephen Spender, C. Day Lewis, Louis MacNeice and others at Oxford, and with Christopher Isherwood down from Cambridge, where Edward Upward had fulfilled a role as left-wing guru not unlike that played by Auden at Oxford. 'Played' seems a fair enough word. Auden seems to have tried on roles rather as he tried on different hats, to test his ideas, his personality or his companions' reactions. He told Stephen Spender, not merely that he *liked* the walk along the canal by the gasworks and the municipal rubbish dump, a believable if unusual preference, but that it was the most *beautiful* in Oxford. And he gave audience to impressionable undergraduates, by appointment, wearing a green eyeshade in a darkened room. The dons were evidently less impressed, for to everyone's astonishment the obviously brilliant young man obtained only a third-class degree. Presumably Auden had spent too much time giving lectures and too little attending them. At any rate, he never suggested that the classification was unfair, nor was he downhearted about it. Great poets – an eminence he had already marked out for himself – do not need good degrees.

If the social awareness of slum conditions lay at the heart of the political work of the Thirties, the early imaginary world seems to come to life again within the metaphysical post-war work. Witness some of the items listed by Auden in his later idea of the Good Society or 'Eden':

Landscape
Limestone uplands like the Pennines plus a small region of igneous rocks with at least one extinct volcano. A precipitous and indented sea-coast.

Oxford gasworks and the river at St Ebbe's in Auden's undergraduate days

20

Climate
British.
Form of Government
Absolute monarchy, elected for life by lot.
Weights and measures
Irregular and complicated. No decimal system.
Economic activities
Lead mining, coal mining, chemical factories, paper mills, sheep farming, truck farming, greenhouse horticulture.
Means of transport
Horses and horse-drawn vehicles, narrow-gauge railways, canal barges, balloons. No automobiles or aeroplanes.

('Reading', *Selected Essays*, p. 13)

In 1939, Auden was claiming that he had always been anti-political:

School life taught me that I was anti-political. I wanted to be left alone . . . . The Enemy was and still is the politician, i.e. the person who wants to organize the lives of others and make them toe the line. I can recognize him instantly, whether as a civil servant, a bishop, a schoolmaster, or a member of a political party . . . .

(*The English Auden*, ed. Mendelson, p. 399)

The left-wing writing and activity of the Thirties seems to be explained, probably truly, by the following:

I have never yet met a Left-Wing intellectual for whom the real appeal of Communism did not lie in its romantic promise that with the triumph of Communism the State shall wither away.

(Ibid. p. 45)

Certainly, there is a ring of truth about the conversation reported by Osborne between Auden and Isherwood on their way to America in 1939, when they found themselves guiltily agreeing that they just couldn't swallow any more of the Popular Front, Party line, or anti-Fascist struggle. 'You know, it just doesn't mean anything for me any more' Isherwood said. A very natural reaction, no doubt, after ten disappointing years of what appeared to be enthusiasm for what appeared to be politics.

The Political Period

By 1922, when he was fifteen, Auden had ceased to believe in religion, and was therefore, as it were, available for the fashionable undergraduate Marxism of his day when he went up to Oxford. It never seems to have become a substitute religion for him, however, as

Cornmarket Street, Oxford, looking north, in the Twenties

it did for so many others. He never actually joined the Party, then or later, and seems to have undertaken communist activities at least in part to please Spender, Isherwood, Day Lewis, and other more enthusiastic friends. The Marxism was part of a more general, psychological theory anyway:

> The progress of man seems to be in a direction away from nature. The development of consciousness may be compared with the breaking away of the child from the Oedipal relation. Just as one must be weaned from one's mother, one must be weaned from the Earth Mother (Unconscious?)
>
> (Journal 1929, in *The English Auden*, ed. Mendelson, p. 298)

Weaned at first scientifically, later theologically, it would seem. Certainly the statement suggests a psychological component – an attempt to break from mother-fixation – in the Thirties' conversion to atheistic Freudianism and Marxism: a suggestion reinforced by the reconversion to High Anglicanism after the death of his mother. But this is not the whole story; that period provided much obvious rational evidence for condemning capitalism, and little that was obvious (until the end of the decade) for condemning Russian communism.

The journal statement is interesting in other ways. In its implicit acceptance of the need to make what is repressed fully conscious, it is in keeping with Auden's Freudianism. Its generality and cool intellectualism accord with the 'airman's' or 'hawk's' view adumbrated in 'Consider' (and elsewhere):

> Consider this and in our time
> As the hawk sees it or the helmeted airman.

But it also accords well enough with Auden's later existentialism (witness Sartre's assertion of the need to be 'pour soi', above and consciously choosing, rather than 'en soi', submerged in the flux of events, in order to be fully human). In this respect, it represents the counter-currents to be found in both the English radical period and the American liberal-conservative one – the counter-currents themselves being constant reminders of the underlying unity that allows apparently quite different works to seem part of the same impressive *opus*. An article he published in Geoffrey Grigson's collection, *The Arts Today* (1935) gives another example of such a counter-current.

> (12) At the root of all disease and sin is a sense of guilt.
> (13) Cure consists in taking away the guilt feeling, in the forgiveness of sins, by confession, the re-living of the experience, and by absolution, understanding its significance.
>
> ('Psychology and Art Today', *The English Auden*, ed. Mendelson, p. 340)

Freudian theory and therapy, but explained in religious terms.

24

In fact, Auden published little political poetry before 1932 – though not so little as his various 'collected' editions (and Mendelson's *Collected Poems*) would lead one to think, for all of them suppress a number of poems; his natural inclinations throughout seem to have been aesthetic, psychological and philosophical rather than political. He envied the great moderns, like Joyce and Eliot, who had come to maturity before World War I so that their rebellion could be purely artistic, not a matter of historical duty as it seemed to his own generation.

During the General Strike of 1926, Auden was one of the minority of Oxbridge undergraduates who worked for the strikers, not against them, but not with any sense of imaginative solidarity. That had to wait upon Hitler's persecution of the Jews after 1933 and the Slump, which began in 1930. At Oxford he was eccentric but not really radical.

When Auden's father agreed to finance a year abroad, after Oxford, in 1928, he chose Berlin, under the liberal Weimar Republic, like Isherwood after him, less out of political interest than for its kinky sex, toleration of homosexuality, and experimental music. He did, however, discover when there the expressionist political drama of Brecht, which strongly influenced the plays he was to write with Isherwood for the Group Theatre, and the political cabaret that inspired a number of songs for Hedli Anderson (a cabaret singer who later became the wife of Louis MacNeice). Possibly even more important, since both politics and religion in Auden tend to be expressed in psychological terms, was his introduction to John Layard, an anthropologist and psychologist who had been first a patient and then a pupil of Homer Lane, an American psychiatrist. Lane took to an extreme certain misconceptions of Freud's doctrines already current. Freud thought that the repression of unwelcome impulses into the subconscious was undesirable because they were then beyond control and were apt to emerge in distorted and perverted forms; made conscious, they could be controlled, and should be. The popular rendering of this idea was simply that impulses should not be repressed. Lane argued in a Lawrentian way that there was a positive duty to indulge them, that self-sacrifice was a subtle and deadly form of selfishness. He also carried Groddeck's and Freud's sensible perception that *some* apparently physical afflictions are really psychological (as in the case of hysterical paralysis) beyond the realms of good sense by asserting that *all* are – an idea that produced many vivid images in Auden's poetry, such as:

> . . . the liar's quinsy
> And the distortions of ingrown virginity.
> (*Poems* 1930. *The English Auden*,
> ed. Mendelson, p. 36)

It also produced much irritation among friends in times of sickness. How far Auden really believed these doctrines is difficult to say; it seems likely that he adopted them largely for their poetical usefulness and social provocativeness. Lane's doctrine of the inhibiting effect of authority and the creativity of social love (again, something assimilable to the later Christianity) seems to have gone deeper. 'Loopy' Layard has one other claim to fame. In an attempt at suicide he put a gun to the roof of his mouth and shot himself right through the head – and survived for another forty years, no loopier than before.

After Berlin, Auden tutored in London and taught at private schools till 1935. His most directly political work is to be found in the poems of these years (which brought him instant fame), the plays (in collaboration with Isherwood), and in the fine poem 'Spain' (later suppressed by the author), a product of the Spanish Civil War. A few weeks' experience of that war, however, seems to have sown the seeds of disillusionment with communism – an experience shared by George Orwell after much deeper and longer involvement, and illuminated brilliantly in *Homage to Catalonia*, an essential background book for this period. Most significantly, Auden found himself to be irrationally shocked at finding all the churches in Barcelona closed.

These years, of course, saw the triumph of Nazism in Germany, the Japanese invasion of Manchuria, Fascist Italy's invasion of Abyssinia, the Slump in England (and indeed in the rest of Europe) and the Depression in America; a time for political protest if ever there was one. In 1932 *New Signatures* appeared (ed. Michael Roberts), in 1936 John Lehmann's influential *New Writing*: in these Auden was the leader of a very sizable school, as these two publications revealed, though many of its members were more politically committed than he was. The voice of this early political poetry often *was* that of the Leader – and both Auden and Isherwood acknowledged that had current youthful fashion been different they could just as easily have been fascist as communist. Indeed, Isherwood, in youthful innocence, did actually write an article for Oswald Mosley's *Action* (in 1931, however; before Mosley's formation of the British Union of Fascists in 1932).

In June 1935 Auden, on the recommendation of Isherwood, who had declined the honour himself, married Thomas Mann's daughter Erika to ensure her escape from Germany. The marriage was not dissolved though it was never consummated, nor did the couple live together. More significantly, for his poetry, he joined the G.P.O. film unit as a writer and assistant director – an experience that had some technical influence on his later poetry.

Travels are the most significant events of the latter half of the decade. Apart from the brief visit to Spain, there was an extended visit to Iceland (July to September) in 1936, the year of the outbreak of the Spanish Civil War, and a trip to, and through China (January to July) in 1938, the year of Hitler's invasion of Austria, and the Munich

Auden and Britten in 1941, when the first performances of their operetta
Paul Bunyan *were being given in New York*

agreement that effectively gave Czechoslovakia to Hitler. Finally, in January 1939, the departure for New York.

The journey to Iceland in the company of Louis MacNeice, like that to China, was subsidised by his publisher Faber and Faber. Auden was attracted to the bleak and extraordinary scenery and by the Icelanders themselves. The weather he found destestable and the food indescribably horrible. But what the journey produced was the marvellous long light-verse 'Letter to Lord Byron', which has nothing whatever to do with Iceland. It does, however, give the first hint of retraction of some of his views:

> Hail to the New World! Hail to those who'll love
> Its antiseptic objects, feel at home
>
> ....
> Preserve me from the Shape of Things to Be.
> (*The English Auden*, ed. Mendelson, pp. 175–6)

A particularly significant comment in the light of the drastic alterations Auden made later to many of those poems of the Thirties not omitted entirely from later collected editions (including Mendelson's, which however prints all these poems in their original form in *The English Auden*). The visit to China, with Isherwood, resulted in *Journey to a War* which included Auden's 'In Time of War' a spendid sonnet sequence with a verse commentary (also much altered later). The fact that Auden and Isherwood never actually caught up with the fighting probably was of benefit to the poetry, for what Auden was good at was not directly reflecting experience but reflecting upon it and this is what these sonnets do.

Meanwhile *Look Stranger!* (1936) had been published (the title, which Auden disliked, having been provided by Faber while he was in Iceland; he titled the American edition *On This Island*). He had written the poems to appear in what is probably his best volume of the decade, *Another Time* (1940). The experimental verse-plays – which anticipated the post-war Theatre of the Absurd in drawing upon charades, music hall, cabaret and panto – had been produced, with a success due more to the period than their intrinsic merits, by Group Theatre: *The Dance of Death* (1934), *The Dog Beneath the Skin* (1936), *On the Frontier* (1938).

In New York, Auden settled in a house in Brooklyn, which he ran as a sort of intellectual commune. The ménage included Salvador Dali, Benjamin Britten, Peter Pears, Gipsy Rose Lee and, among others, Chester Kallman with whom Auden was to spend most of the rest of his life, though as a friend rather than 'spouse' after the first few years. He proved surprisingly efficient at the job, devising menus, hiring and firing servants, standing no nonsense about the rents, having meals served on the dot and being very strict with latecomers – a strictness that increased with the years, till he would turn out the invited guest

Auden and Kallman at the Venice P.E.N. conference in 1949, photographed by Stephen Spender

who had not finished his coffee and brandy before Auden's nine o'clock bedtime (the prerequisite of a very early morning start). All this parallels an increasing technical concern with poetics, and a belief that even a lyric poet should consider himself a craftsman not a visionary genius.

He had always been aware of the danger of becoming so fascinated by the process of decay that one might lose the will to eliminate it; now he became doubtful whether it could be eliminated without something worse befalling society. In 1940 he began teaching in New York, attended church again and, reconverted, took the Anglican communion in the October of that year. He was still to write much social poetry, but the 'political' period (something of an overstatement anyway) was over. From now on his social poetry was to be anti-ideological, anti-political.

The Religious Period

In a sense this period too is misnamed, for poems that are not specifically religious, indeed not religious at all, far outnumber those that are. In fact, after a period of convertite enthusiasm, ending about 1950, there is almost no specifically religious poetry, apart from 'Horae Canonicae'. By the time he had digested his conversion he had become relaxed and tolerant – nor did it seem to affect his personality and behaviour at all, in spite of his assertion of having once been possessed by demonic powers (perhaps the effect of the amphetamines and increasing quantities of strong drink he took.) Osborne reports, for instance, that though he came to accept that homosexuality was a sin he cheerfully went on committing homosexual acts. The likelihood is that in this period too Auden's belief was more intellectual than emotional, extreme out of zest rather than zeal. At any rate, he came to find matter for comedy in the same principles that brought Kierkegaard to despair. If the world and its inhabitants are both fallen and blessed, and therefore people are 'human' only if frail and inconsistent; if the divine is necessarily unknowable, and faith therefore blind; and if *any* course of action will be imperfect since man is fallen; then nothing in earthly life is of fundamental importance – so a serene human comedy is as possible an attitude to it as existentialist *angst*. And in fact there is more poetry of that kind in this 'pessimistic' period than in the communistic period that ought, theoretically, to have been more optimistic. There is, then, a sense in which the later non-religious poetry is in one way or another, strongly or tenuously, related to the background of religious belief – though Auden himself indicates a complicating factor:

> Whatever their personal faith
> all poets, as such,
> are polytheists.
> (*Collected Poems*, ed. Mendelson, p. 666)

Indeed, Auden puts both periods in capsule form in one of his last poems, 'A Thanksgiving':

> Then, without warning, the whole
> Economy suddenly crumbled:
>   there, to instruct me, was *Brecht*.
>
> Finally, hair-raising things
> that Hitler and Stalin were doing
>   forced me to think about God.
>
> Why was I sure they were wrong?
> Wild *Kierkegaard*, *Williams*, and *Lewis*
>   guided me back to belief.
>
> Now, as I mellow in years
> and home in a bountiful landscape,
>   Nature allures me again.
>   (Ibid. p. 671)

Throughout Auden's life there runs a thread of outstanding nature poetry, different from any that we are accustomed to. But, again, that of the later period, though characteristically Audenesque and thus not incongruous with that of the earlier, is subtly affected by the Christian existentialist dogmas he had chosen to adopt. So there is as much justification for styling this period 'religious' as for styling the pre-war period 'political' – and as little.

From 1940 to 1973, the year of his death, Auden's life is largely a record of ceaseless work, increasingly punctuated by medals, prizes, international awards. He had always been a rapid worker of outstanding technical ability:

> You could say to him 'Please write me a double ballade on the virtues of a certain brand of toothpaste, which also contains at least ten anagrams on the names of well-known politicians and of which the refrain is as follows . . .' Within twenty-four hours, your ballade would be ready – and it would be good.
>
> (Isherwood: 'Some notes on the early poetry' in *W. H. Auden: A Tribute*, ed. Spender, p. 75)

Now he became not only an even faster worker and studier, but a more disciplined and careful one ('God how careless I used to be'). He grew even less interested in possessions or appearance, more in favour of sanity and commonsense – rather in contradiction to his ostensible theological beliefs. He appeared on television but never watched it, deplored photography ('It just ain't art') and biography – though he loved gossip and, indeed, claimed it to be the foundation of literary art: observing and telling. Possibly the extraordinary hard work was another drug for the underlying melancholy that suffuses many of the poems, even comic ones.

From 1940–1945 he taught at various colleges (see Biographical Chronology) and at the same time wrote the long theological, soul-searching poems that so dismayed his admirers. Of *For the Time Being* (1944), an existentialist Christmas oratorio, it is true there is little to be praised. To anyone not enraptured by recherché theological problems it must appear intolerably pious and pompous, and even longer than it is. *New Year Letter* (1941) (*The Double Man* in the U.S.) may be commended as tour-de-force in that it very clearly versifies a rather complex metaphysic, and does also contain one or two passages of great intelligence and perceptiveness, especially on the nature of art. *The Sea and the Mirror* is notable for some wonderfully accomplished poetry in extremely difficult verse-forms, and for the intricate prose of 'Caliban's Address to the Audience', which Auden thought to be the best thing he had ever written. Certainly it displays a superlative cleverness that must be admired even by those most sceptical about Auden's later ideas and beliefs. *The Age of Anxiety* (1947) for most will seem a long-winded unsatisfactory amalgam of psychology and theology, in which the characters have no life and all speak alike, but it does contain one or two beautiful, and detachable poems, and again much subtle if suspect cleverness. In addition to this monumental body of work Auden also wrote the libretto for Britten's *Paul Bunyan* and, as always, a considerable body of articles and reviews.

In 1945, he spent a few months with the U.S. forces in occupied Germany as a civilian research officer (ranking as major) in the Morale Division of the U.S. Strategic Bombing Survey, a post that his command of the language – which he eventually perfected – made him suitable for, if nothing else did. For the first time since 1939 he was able to visit England again, now under the first effective Labour Government. Once, presumably, this would have attracted him. He returned to capitalist America, resumed university teaching, and in 1946 became a naturalised citizen of the U.S.A. In 1948 he visited Ischia, an island in the Bay of Naples, where he rented a house for the spring and summer of every year from 1949 to 1957, thus keeping in touch with European culture. These years saw the publication of two 'collected' editions, and *Nones* (1951) and *The Shield of Achilles* (1955), one of his finest volumes.

In 1955 Auden settled at 77 St Mark's Place, New York where he remained till his last brief stay at Oxford. In 1958, with the proceeds of an Italian literary prize, he bought a converted farmhouse in Kirchstetten, near Vienna, where he spent every spring and summer for the rest of his life – a purchase celebrated in the poems of *About the House* (1965). In 1956 he had been elected Professor of Poetry at Oxford, a largely honorary post requiring the delivery of only three lectures during each of the five years of tenure. Auden, however, when in residence, made himself available to any student who wished to talk with him, and was prepared to give much time and patience to young poets. The best works of this period are *Homage to Clio* (1960) and the collection of prose essays *The Dyer's Hand* (1962).

This settled, hardworking life, geared to an inflexible daily and seasonal pattern, was briefly interrupted in 1964 by a second visit to Iceland – now as one of the royal family of literature – and six months in Berlin, as a member of an artists-in-residence programme sponsored by the Ford Foundation. In 1972, however, came what Auden had increasingly longed for, the chance to return before his death to the country of his birth, to live in a 'grace and favour' cottage in the grounds of Christ Church. But the final return visit was not to turn out so triumphal as the years of his professorship. Auden was still the gifted teacher he had always been, whether at school or university level; but he had aged and degenerated considerably, worn out by years of incessant writing and lecturing and by the stimulants required to

Ischia, an island in the Bay of Naples, where Auden spent spring and summer from 1949 to 1957

33

sustain the pressure; the elephant-hide skin of his later years was more deeply seamed than ever. Though few of the dire world events from 1940 onwards were reflected directly in the verse of those three decades – it concerned itself with more general issues – he seems to have become a deeply disillusioned and saddened man. Seeing everything in perspective he had come to see how small everything could seem. He was famous and honoured – and lonely, deliberately, penitentially so. Moreover, students had changed; the new generation was fashionably 'anti-élitist' and tended to prefer ill-made verse to well-made. On 29 September Wystan Hugh Auden died in Vienna on the way back to Oxford from Kirchstetten. He was buried in 'a grave of honour' in Kirchstetten churchyard, and the village street was renamed Audenstrasse. His true remains, however, consist of the great body of work he left behind. Much of the early work is craggy and obscure, much of the later so unbuttoned as to verge on genial chat, but the best has the consummate ease that comes only from the most practised and refined art, the art that conceals art.

2 The Political and Historical Context

Pre-War

Bracketed by the Slump and the Second World War, the decade in which Auden rocketed to fame, the Thirties, has a uniquely self-contained look about it. An illusory look, of course; for the Thirties grew out of the Twenties as surely as our Eighties – already (1983) frighteningly reminiscent of the Thirties – have in part resulted from the cumulative errors and disasters, national and international, that preceded them. Moreover, the Twenties was the decade of Auden's formative teenage and undergraduate years. Like the Thirties, they were years of economic decline and class struggle, overshadowed eerily from two directions, the war past and the war ever more likely to come. The famous frivolity of the Twenties – characteristic, anyway, only of the fairly privileged – was not so much an expression of *joie de vivre*, or even *de survivre*, as of desperation. Traces of it remain (and are to be discerned in Auden's early work) in the thickening gloom of the Thirties.

The colossal cost of the First World War vastly accelerated a British decline already in evidence before it began. A poorer nation could not, or at any rate did not, provide the promised 'homes fit for heroes to live in'; the 'war to end war' was immediately followed by worldwide disturbances, including British fighting in Russia and Ireland; the pre-war class-system and its great disparity of wealth remained unchanged, unemployment was rife, economic recovery slow. Auden, at a public school, was cushioned against most of the disillusion and discontent of the time, but was not entirely ignorant of it, and when it culminated in the General Strike of 1926, forsook his class and worked for the strikers. Moreover, since Germany had been hit even harder by the war, he encountered in the Berlin of 1928 a graphic heightening of England's troubles. Italy, of course, had been a Fascist state, under Mussolini, since 1922. The Thirties, then, represented a dramatic change in degree, not in kind.

The decade opened disastrously as the tidal wave of the Wall Street crash of 1929, due mainly to financial gambling, hit Britain (and the rest of Europe, also in debt to America) in 1930. The endemic economic crisis of the Twenties turned into the Great Depression or Slump. The crash instantly put an end to American loans to Europe and led to the calling in of wartime loans (which the Allies attempted to recoup by way of reparations from Germany, thus helping to push that country into Nazism). This led to a drying up of purchasing power all over the world, to recession, and thus increased the likelihood of wars for gain (as in the case of Japan) or *lebensraum* (living space, as alleged by Germany). Britain had already been hard hit by American and Japanese competition, by the dislocation of international trade during the war, and paradoxically by Germany's payments of reparations of kind – shiploads of free coal, for example, further harming an already struggling British coal industry. The general raising of tariff barriers, too, caused disproportionate harm to countries like Britain that were not self-sufficient in food and therefore had to export to survive. No National Government, then, by any sort of policy could have completely solved the problems of the Slump, as its ultimate causes were extra-national – a fact reflected by a sense of impotence in the face of uncontrollable forces, which seeps into much poetry that is overtly radical and positive. This sense may well be one reason why Auden was not alone in turning eventually from politics to the consolation of metaphysics. The Conservative ('Coalition') government, however, made the problems worse by taking what is clearly the best course for individuals in such a situation but, at any rate according to Maynard Keynes, whose doctrines proved successful in practice after the Second World War, the worst for nations. They economised. Public expenditure was drastically reduced, wages and salaries severely cut – with the result that people had less purchasing power, so that many firms collapsed, unable to sell their products, more people lost their jobs thus further reducing purchasing power, and the vicious circling set in that culminated in a peak of three and three-quarter million unemployed in Britain by 1932 (when Auden was a school teacher in England). Germany had six million unemployed, the U.S. twelve million.

The suffering was not, however, uniformly distributed. Indeed, for those with money these were good years. Internal prices went down as purchasing power declined, so that the well-to-do could live better. In fact, the standard of living even of the *average* man, outside the depressed areas of the North and South Wales, actually improved during the Thirties. But what added a new kind of guilt to that already suffered by the more sensitive of the middle-classes of Auden's age at having been safe during the war and ignorant and unimaginative about its horror was the stark disparity between haves and have-nots, between the gentry of the Home Counties and the grim misery of towns like Jarrow and those of the Rhondda where almost the whole of the male population was unemployed.

If, however, this sense of alienation of having been neither warrior nor worker but a comfortable unimaginative bourgeois, with a privileged education, was the main impulse driving middle-class poets to Marxism or near Marxism, rather as a faith than an economic and political theory, it was not the only one. The Labour Government – not in any case with a working majority – split in 1931 over financial policy and was replaced by a so-called Coalition or National

Government consisting of a few renegade Labourites and an overwhelming Tory majority. Disunity in the Labour Party, combined with incompetence and hard heartedness in the National Government, persuaded many people of humane and liberal but left-wing sympathics to support the Communist Party. Furthermore, Russia appeared to be the only country to be weathering the Slump. The fact that improvement left her peoples still far worse off than those in the West, and the facts of bureaucratic muddle and tyranny, were little known and, where known, were excused on grounds of initial backwardness and political necessity. Finally, Communism seemed to be the only real opposition to Nazism. So, although there is undoubtedly much truth in Auden's claim that he and his contemporaries were really more interested in psychology than politics, in unmasking the bourgeoisie, Marx came increasingly, but always uneasily, to be united with Freud in the new myth that formed a ground for much of Auden's poetry in this decade.

As the economic depression slowly improved, the international situation steadily worsened: from the Japanese invasion of Manchuria in 1931, through the invasion of Abyssinia by Italy (1935), the Rhineland (1936), Austria (1938), Czechoslovakia (1939) by Germany, to the outbreak of World War II when Hitler invaded Poland – and Russia took the opportunity of attacking Finland, in the autumn of 1939.

In 1932, when unemployment was at its peak, Sir Oswald Mosley founded the British Union of Fascists (which had acquired a paid-up membership of 20,000 by 1934). In 1933, the Nazis came to power in Germany (on a minority vote) and Germany left the League of Nations. In 1933 Hitler became Chancellor of Germany – and dictator, by killing off possible rivals amongst his colleagues on the Night of the Long Knives. Japan followed Germany's example and also left the League of Nations – and advanced from Manchuria into China proper. In 1934 the great Disarmament Conference, convened at Geneva in 1932, was adjourned indefinitely, as no nation was prepared to take action over Germany's illegal rearming. In the following year Britain and France made it clear that they were not going to work any system of collective security or damage their economies by imposing crippling sanctions on Italy to put an end to its Abyssinian adventure. In 1936, however, something *was* done when the fascist general Franco led an armed uprising against the properly elected Republican Government (far from left-wing, and in fact under constant communist attack before the civil war broke out). Britain and France helped Franco (and incidentally Hitler and Mussolini) by agreeing to non-intervention, and enforcing it, while Hitler and Mussolini ignored the agreement. This led to Franco's getting a great deal of aid overland from the fascist countries while the Republican Government was prevented from obtaining arms from overseas by

British and French naval patrols. Russia refused aid until the Communist Party had obtained control of the Republican side – one of the facts causing disenchantment with communism among left-wing intellectuals. Another was the Russian show trials of 1937, though for most the breaking-point came with the cynical Russo-German pact made in 1939 at the very time that England and France, with some reluctance admittedly, were engaged in negotiations for a united front with Russia. A secret protocol to the pact apportioned various eastern European states between the two powers; Russia was to have Estonia, Finland, Latvia, eastern Poland and part of Rumania, Germany to have Lithuania and western Poland. By April 1939 fascism was triumphant in Spain; in September Nazi and Soviet armies met at Brest Litovsk in mid-Poland. Japan was master of China, Italy seized Albania, Russia Finland. What Auden called 'a low, dishonest decade' had come to the end that all had so long dreaded. Auden's political commitment, and with it his political poetry, had also come to an end.

Spain

1936 stands as the turning-point of the decade and a crucial year for the 'New Country' or left-wing poets, of whom Auden was the leading light. The Spanish Civil War crystallised the complexities of the period into an almost mythical simplicity. The nations of the world were slowly dragging themselves out of the Slump; on the other hand they seemed to be rushing like the Gadarene swine to the disaster of another World War. Could that downward rush be halted? Now was the time for taking sides, even for taking action. A sizable portion of the Left became war-minded, feeling it necessary to stop the dictators in their tracks before they became strong enough to transfer the Spanish rehearsal to the world stage. The issues seemed to become clear-cut – and certainly 'Spain' did dramatically increase the polarisation of England. The Right strongly supported non-intervention, the extreme Right openly advocated fascism. Many of the Left, from both the working-class and the middle-class, joined the International Brigade and went to fight for the Republican side. Orwell, who was amongst them, wrote in his essay 'Inside the Whale': 'Nobody I knew who went to Spain during the Civil War, who was not a dyed-in-the-wool Stalinist, came back with his illusions intact.' *Homage to Catalonia* (1938), a fascinating inside account, details his disillusion – not with the Republican cause in general but with the Russian-dominated communist section which finally managed to take it over. Auden's and Spender's briefer contact with the war, too, seems to have diminished their enthusiasm for communism (though in no way lessening their detestation of fascism). At home, the Friends of Spain favoured the Republicans, the Friends of Nationalist Spain, the rebels. The press divided almost equally, and innumerable pamphlets competed for attention. In this year the Left Book Club was formed. Soon attracting 50,000 members, it became a powerful influence. Henceforth, if the Right dominated Government, the Left dominated public opinion.

The polarisation was not, however, universal. The major part of the British people simply wished to keep out of war at all costs. Hence the popularity of the appeasement policy – probably a much more enlightened policy than it is now given credit for. It had the misfortune to come up against a national leader, in the person of Hitler, who could hardly be considered sane by any normal standards. To most people it never became clear that pacifism, in the circumstances of the day, must be absolutist or nothing. One could not logically advocate 'collective security' against the dictators *and* oppose rearmament and the use of force. But over 100,000 people did take the more logical stance, by joining the Peace Pledge Union (founded in 1934) and pledging themselves never to fight in a war.

In that they were communists, or fellow-travellers, Auden and the poets associated with him were logically but uncomfortably aligned with the war party. The importance of the Spanish Civil War for their poetry, however, is not that it made it more warlike, but rather that it gave it a sharper focus. Until that time the 'social' poetry of the Thirties, including that of Auden, had tended to be new and exciting but bitty. The myths of Romanticism and Christianity, so long the standby of literature, had been replaced by a creakily-working model put together from *Boys' Magazine* stories, spy novels, Norse sagas, and a selection of the doctrines of Freud and Marx. The attempt to make a new myth fit for the new age, to break, in particular, from the bookish and somewhat snobbish modes of Eliot, Pound and Yeats, gave their poetry a certain liveliness and sense of relevance: but since it had not been assimilated into lived experience these qualities were too often accompanied by undergraduate showing off of knowledge recently acquired and not fully understood, mystification, and pretentiousness. The Spanish Civil War gave the new myth drama, simplicity, and above all a more evident and urgent relevance:

> On that arid square, that fragment nipped off from hot
> Africa, soldered so crudely by inventive Europe,
> > On that tableland scored by rivers,
> Our fever's menacing shapes are precise and alive.
> ('Spain 1937', *The English Auden*, ed. Mendelson, p. 210)

A stanza typical of Auden's special qualities. There is the distant overview, as if the poet were a general poring over a map; the swiftly characterising adjectives ('arid', 'inventive') that seem to seize on the essential distinguishing feature; the hint of inherent violence in 'scored'; an evocation of a world in delirium through 'fever'; and of course the political perception, put as paradox, in the idea of Spain's fever being 'ours'.

Auden, Isherwood and Spender in the early Thirties

In a sense, a certain relevance and relative coherence had underlain the quirkiness of the new myth from the start – as indeed must be the case if any unifying framework of ideas is to count as 'myth' Psychology, politics and economics could be, and were, woven into the same poem firstly by taking the notions of a quest, a border, or a battle to have both a political and a psychological reference; secondly, by

40

applying two psychological theories not to individuals (or not only to individuals) but to the nation; Lane's and Groddeck's theory that physical illnesses were the outward and visible signs of an inward disgrace was combined with Freud's theory of subconscious violence below the respectable surface, sometimes indeed expressing itself through respectable manners and morality, of neurosis and repression given away by small symptoms, of Eros twisted and perverted by convention and tradition (especially into a love of possessions), and of the death-wish, the desire of living matter to return to the passivity of the inanimate. Both the Slump and international politics, then, could be graphically shown in terms of a sick country, the behaviour of the ruling classes as neurotic, even expressive of a death-wish. Witness, for example, one of the expurgated stanzas of 'A Summer Night 1933':

> For what by nature and by training
> We loved, has little strength remaining
>
> . . . .
> It has no wish to live.
> (*Look Stranger!*, 1936, *The English Auden*, ed. Mendelson, p. 136)

Such a myth, naive in essence but fresh and brash, could be adapted to cover an immense range of new reference, new views; it could be complicated, made a vehicle for farce or satire; it could unite the personal and the political; speak of capitalism and socialism without the prosiness of economic analysis. What it lacked was drama and concentration of feeling. Those came with the Spanish Civil War. When that was lost, all seemed lost. Auden moved to a New World, literally and mythically, and to a poetry above politics.

Post-War

For this period the cultural and philosophical context is much more important for an understanding of Auden's poetry than the political and historical context. Whatever the ultimate cause of his conversion to Christianity, disillusion with the Munich agreement and the Russo-German pact was certainly a contributory factor. But if the world was beyond redemption it did not follow that the individual need be. In his new myth the quest was entirely an inner one:

> In theory they were sound on Expectation,
> Had there been situations to be in;
> Unluckily they were their situation
> ('The Quest', 1940, *Collected Poems*, ed. Mendelson, p. 224)

A fallen world clearly could not be changed fundamentally. Indeed, on Kierkegaardian principles it *should* not be, since only by disaster will most men be brought to take the irrational 'leap in the dark' to Faith. Moreover, from the infinite distance of a divine perspective even the

Auden, Day Lewis and Spender at the Venice P.E.N. conference in 1949, photographed by Natasha Spender

gravest material events are indistinguishable from the most trivial: 'the lover's nip and the grip of the torturer's tongs are all – ask Ariel – variants of one common type' (*The Sea and the Mirror, III*). So, while the earth-shattering events of the Second World War were perpetrated, from the Blitz to Hiroshima, Auden was wrestling fascinatedly with theological problems in the sequence of long poems *New Year Letter* (1940), *For the Time Being* (1941–2), *The Sea and the Mirror* (1942–4), and *The Age of Anxiety* (1944–6). If the major events of the post-war period are reflected at all in his poetry – and some of them are – it is indirectly. The formation of U.N.O., N.A.T.O., and the E.E.C., the Cold War, the Korean War, the Vietnamese War, the Arab-Israeli wars, the Pill, the space missions, and so on, all go unremarked, or at any rate are seen *sub specie aeternitatis*, subsumed under some more general consideration. So the 'Moon Landing' immediately moves into reflections on the basic nature of men and women, of today's and Homer's heroes, hubris, irreverence and history – and, mostly, contemporary relevance is even more indirect and subordinate than that. The following lines from 'Woods' refer not to any particular society or exploitation or calamity; the particular is subordinated to a general reflection on Man and Nature:

> A small grove massacred to the last ash,
> An oak with heart-rot, give away the show:
> This great society is going smash;
> They cannot fool us with how fast they go ...

Similarly, 'The Fall of Rome' (*Collected Poems*, Mendelson, p. 257) by mingling modern and classical references lifts the poem to the level of metaphysical pondering on the disintegration of all great civilisations, and concludes by contrasting them with the great natural simplicity that will outlast them, and beside which they are found absurdly wanting:

> Altogether elsewhere, vast
> Herds of reindeer move across
> Miles and miles of golden moss,
> Silently and very fast.

Moreover, Auden had now come to believe not only that poetry does not make anything happen but that it is arrogant of a poet to try to make it do so. The poet's business is to rise above the mundane, play games with words, entertain, and unpompously, unpreachingly lift the hearts, minds, and spirits of his readers. How far he has reversed his earlier attitudes can be judged from one stanza of his Phi Beta Kappa poem, Harvard 1946, 'Under Which Lyre' (significantly if ironically subtitled 'A Reactionary Tract for the Times'):

> Thou shalt not answer questionnaires
> Or quizzes upon World-Affairs,
>   Nor with compliance
> Take any test. Thou shalt not sit
> With statisticians nor commit
>   A social science.

(Ibid. p. 262)

By God's grace or with luck such unpretentious work might, rarely, express a great and moving truth – but such truths were by definition more than merely contemporary; they were truths of man's essential being, of the essential nature of the Good Society, or of the nature of Nature. And minor entertaining or stimulating truths, or even untruths, were also to be valued in their kind.

It was perhaps a natural progression in one for whom, at his most socially committed, psychology had always taken precedence over politics and cheerfulness had always been apt to break in.

3   The Cultural and Philosophical Context

The English Period

> Coming out of me living is always thinking,
> Thinking changing and changing living.
> ('1929', *Collected Poems*, ed. Mendelson, p. 50)

These lines, along with a good many others, suggest that Auden anticipated the changes to come in both his thinking and living. All those changes came about in consequence of that major transfer of belief, from atheistic Freudian Marxism to existentialist Episcopalian liberalism which coincided with his transfer of habitat from London to New York. Their nature is interestingly exemplified in the changes made in certain poems for the *Collected Shorter Poems* of 1950 (not to mention the many significant omissions). Here, for instance, are two examples from the verse commentary of *Journey to a War* (1939) (*The English Auden*, p. 262).

> Man can improve himself but never will be perfect (1939)
> Man can improve but never will himself be perfect (1950)

At first, that is to say, man's improvement is said to be in his own hands, but he will never attain perfection. Later, it is implied man can be perfect but not by his own merely human efforts. The poem concludes:

> Rally the lost and trembling forces of the will,
> Gather them up and let them loose upon the earth,
>
> Till they construct at last a human justice,
> The contribution of our star, within the shadow
> Of whose uplifting, loving and constraining power
> All other reasons may rejoice and operate (1939)
>
> Till, as the contribution of our star, we follow
> The clear instructions of that Justice in the shadow
> Of Whose uplifting, loving and constraining power
> All other reasons may rejoice and operate (1950)

A specifically human justice is turned into a divine Justice, the earth is to follow heavenly instructions rather than make its own order, and in the one case non-human reasons are to be subordinate to human justice, in the other human reasons are to be subordinate to divine Justice. A little skilful plastic surgery, and the poem is made to say the opposite of what it used to. Much the same thing happens to 'A

Summer Night 1933' (published 1936). Three stanzas towards the end are omitted from the 1950 version. The first satirises the metaphysical distress of privileged people behind creepered walls, unaware of the hungry and wretched outside. The next speaks of inexorable forces of change, and the third of a death-wish in their privileged culture. The poem then speaks of a flood that will sweep everything away and prepare the ground for a new order. In 1936 there followed an exhortation to welcome the new order:

> May this for which we dread to lose
> Our privacy need no excuse.

In 1950 (with the anti-bourgeois stanzas omitted) these lines read as follows:

> May these delights we dread to lose,
> This privacy, need no excuse.

Now, one should *not* feel guilty about a privileged culture.

These examples, which could be matched by many more, indicate either directly or by implication a series of linked changes of view: from a belief in a planned society to a belief in liberal individualism, from a belief in deterministic forces, historical and psychological, governing us do what we may, to a belief in free will, a future resulting from ethical choices for which we are responsible, and from being, so to speak, for the Managers and against the Establishment to being the reverse.

That these changes are not really as extreme as they appear has already been suggested. They may be extreme as changes of opinion – but poetry is a great deal more than opinion, and Auden's is essentially cool and contemplative in both periods, speculative rather than passionate, inviting not zealous participation but zestful consideration ('Consider this and in our time/As the hawk sees it . . .'). Amongst the reasons for change were no doubt emotional ones, personal and political: shock at his mother's death, disillusion with Russia, the sense of failure to influence history, boredom with what came eventually to seem leftist clichés. One reason was certainly that of intellectual curiosity, of trying out a new set of ideas – and, one must add, shocking ideas in their day. In his early years Auden delighted in snook-cocking, extravagance, and nonsense; it is questionable whether he ever wholly lost that delight. Certainly he chose as extreme a brand of theology as he had chosen of psychology, both going at times so far beyond commonsense as to approach nonsense; so that stimulation and irritation may well be produced by the same poem. Moreover, Auden was always an eccentric, suspect, improperly individualistic communist – something easily transmuted into the uncharacteristically tolerant, sinful, humorous Christian existentialist he became. So, too, the early ideas that love should transcend the personal to embrace society at large could easily evolve into the Christian idea of non-sexual love. It is no accident that in some cases Auden could revise an atheistic Freudian poem into a Christian existentialist one simply by turning 'love' and 'father' into 'Love' and 'Father'.

However, what we are really concerned with in this section is neither Auden's apparent contradictoriness nor his underlying consistency but rather the surrounding ideas and influences that surface from time to time in his poetry (or are glimpsed beneath the surface) and may help in appreciating it. One reservation needs to be made: Auden never swallowed any ideas uncritically, and what he did swallow he digested pretty thoroughly into his own ideas and personality.

Auden's Study of Freud

Before 1914 the old framework of religious, ethical and economic beliefs had been shaken by the works of Darwin, Marx, Frazer and Freud, the framework of literary beliefs by the work of Eliot and Pound, to which was shortly to be added the iconoclasm of dada and surrealism. The disillusion of the Twenties and the disasters of the Thirties provoked an attempt to destroy what remained of those frameworks – an attempt shared by Auden more in the field of ideas than in his poetic practice; for though much of what he said, and something of the way he said it, was at odds with traditional poetry, he was not a modernist (save briefly at the beginning, under the influence of Eliot).

Auden's primary rebellion seems to have been in the area of the personal life rather than the social. Hence the influence of Freud precedes that of Marx. Though neither so extreme as certain associates and followers, like Groddeck and Lane (both of whom, as we have noted, influenced Auden) nor so 'permissive' as Lawrence and many others took him to be, Freud's effect on what remained of the old framework of belief was cataclysmic. He provided ideal ammunition for a generation made deeply sceptical, even cynical, about that framework by what it had supported, the senseless slaughter of the Great War. Both in general and in particular Freud was shocking.

In general, he undermined the traditional assumptions of the dominance of free-will and reason in man by arguing – as did Groddeck – that we are 'lived' by unknown and uncontrollable forces in the Id, that there is no such thing as psychological freedom (an idea obviously parallel to the Marxist idea of our being determined by the forces of history and economics). That being so, it follows that one should be both more ruthless and less censorious (equally a consequence of Marxist theory), for those in the wrong are neither blamable nor fundamentally changeable. Again, Freud casts doubt on the objectivity and accuracy of perception, and of course on traditional concepts of heroism and selfless goodness, by suggesting the constant presence of unconscious bias and motive. Above all, Freud shocked the older generation by making the sexual drive as all-important as Marx made economics.

In particular, Freud's evidence that God was a rationalised projection of the small child's experience of the father, was a further blow to religion; his attribution of sexuality to infants, a blow to sentimentality; his argument for a deeply underlying death-wish, a blow to confidence. All grist to Auden's mill in the Thirties. His spendid tribute to Freud on his death in 1939 concludes:

> One rational voice is dumb. Over his grave
> the household of Impulse mourns one deeply loved:
>   sad is Eros, builder of cities,
>   and weeping anarchic Aphrodite.
>   ('In Memory of Sigmund Freud')

The same poem, however, indicates why Freud should later on be found to be assimilable to Auden's later liberalism and Christianity (though he really fits no more easily with the bigoted Kierkegaard than he does with Marx). The positive side to Freud's influence was the vast extension of charity, tolerance, sympathy, understanding, and life-enhancement:

> Hate and his dingy clientele
> are still alive but in a world he changed
> simply by looking back with no false regrets;
>   all he did was to remember
>   like the old and be honest like children.
>
> He wasn't clever at all: he merely told
> the unhappy Present to recite the Past
>   like a poetry lesson till sooner
>   or later it faltered at the line where
>
> long ago the accusations had begun,
> and suddenly knew by whom it had been judged,
>   and how rich life had been and how silly,
>   and was life-forgiven and more humble,
>
> able to approach the Future as a friend
> without a wardrobe of excuses, without
>   a set mask of rectitude or an
>   embarrassing over-familiar gesture.
>
> No wonder the ancient cultures of conceit
> in his technique of unsettlement foresaw
>   the fall of princes, the collapse of
>   their lucrative patterns of frustration:

> if he succeeded, why, the Generalised Life
> would become impossible, the monolith
>   of State be broken and prevented
>   the co-operation of avengers.
>
> Of course they called on God, but he went his way
> down among the lost people like Dante, down
>   to the stinking fosse where the injured
>   lead the ugly life of the rejected,
>
> and showed us what evil is, not, as we thought,
> deeds that must be punished, but our lack of faith,
>   our dishonest mood of denial.
>   the concupiscence of the oppressor.
>   (*Collected Poems*, ed. Mendelson, p. 216)

In spite of the suggestion that religion is the propaganda arm of the Establishment ('Of course they called on God'), it is evident from these lines that a certain near-religious element was latent in the 'English' Auden. Freud is approved as a saviour, humbleness is approved, and evil is associated with lack of faith (admittedly, as yet with a small 'f'). The obvious approval of breaking 'the monolith of State', too, points to the future – as well as tending to confirm Auden's statement that the attraction of communism was partly based on Marx's remark in passing that the State would eventually wither away under communism.

Auden's Study of Marx

Freud and Marx, though immensely powerful influences on Auden, were very different from him. They were brilliantly original, independent, and inflexible thinkers slowly and doggedly pursuing their ideas of the truth. Auden was something of a magpie-thinker – equally brilliant but not original; swift, adaptable, and ready to pick up anything that glittered. Not, in any strict sense, a thinker at all, but a poet ready to pounce on any material suitable for his particularly airy kind of nest, any bit of mirror that would reflect his experience. In consequence, the influence of Marx becomes rather Freudian; or rather, Auden adapted Marx to suit what he had taken from Freud (itself adapted to the more extreme and provocative Lane and Lawrence); in each case the needs of his poetic vision – *his* view and presentation of perceptions of life – taking precedence over academic completeness and objectivity.

It is doubtful whether Auden knew or cared much about Marx's economic theory. Questions of surplus value, methods of production, and the distribution of profits are too technical to make good material for poetry, and they do not feature in Auden's verse. Revolution, however, does feature, but rather as a beneficial storm or flood clearing the air and renewing the soil – ambiguous metaphors interpretable psychologically as easily as sociologically. The blood, chaos, destruction and suffering of real revolutions are not imaginatively envisaged – but then Auden had almost as strong a tendency to view things *sub specie aeternitatis* (from the eternal viewpoint) in his political as in his religious period. More important to Auden, anyway, was Marx's theory of man's alienation under the capitalist system. Since this was at once an alienation of man from his work and its products – of which he experiences only a small part – *and* from his own essential nature, it could be assimilated to Freudian doctrines of repression, split personality, and socially induced neurosis. Marx could thus be combined with Freud to extend the adolescent and undergraduate Mortmere fantasy* concocted by Auden, Isherwood and Upward into the viable poetic myth described under the 'Political and Historical Context' (p. 39–41). What had begun as a sort of gang joke, an attack on a vague Enemy – the schoolmaster, or don, or adult authority in general – could be given some social breadth or relevance. The enemy became the bourgeois Establishment, sick and neurotic both personally and as the 'head' of a sick country. Economic and political madness could be dramatised in mythic personal terms. Add to this, matter from spy stories and detective novels, Freudianised and Marxified in so far as it could provide metaphors either for the adventure of changing society or for fighting battles within the self, or metaphors for the Freudian and Marxist analyses which saw deep significance in tiny clues and oddities – add this, and you have an up-to-date way of dramatising material that had rarely been the subject of poetry since the Romantic period (*c.* 1790–1830). True, such a myth was neither accurate nor useful as social analysis, or for that matter, personal analysis. But the poet's task – in so far as he is trying to be more than merely self-expressive – is something other than that. It is to render the public mind amenable to such prose analysis, to make it receptive to new ways of seeing and feeling; or more generally, as Shelley said, his task is not to give information so much as to 'awaken and enlarge the mind itself'.

Auden's Myth

The myth in fact rarely purports to purvey, even metaphorically, any serious analysis. Dream, psychological case-histories, nonsense-verse, fairy stories, and opera (the serious art nearest to nonsense) also play their part as influences, so that farce, fantasy, and caricature contribute to keeping priggishness and preaching at a distance (usually, though

*Discussed in Isherwood's *Lions and Shadows*, Hogarth, 1937.

not always, successfully). The medicine is to be taken sweetened, the public to be entertained as well as shocked or instructed. Some poems are entirely fantastical, though probably none is wholly unserious; some are wholly serious, though probably none is entirely unfantastical. So, too, elements of the myth tend to be distributed in varying proportions throughout the political poems. It is never expressed as a whole, any more than the full doctrines of Christianity are to be found in traditional poems which use it as a system of shorthand reference. On the contrary, this or that element crops up here or there, and bit by bit the reader learns how much of the rest, quite unsystematised anyway, is to be taken as relevant in the particular case. It cannot be too strongly emphasised, furthermore, that political poems do not form the bulk of Auden's work even in this period – though love poems and other non-political poems are usually emotionally tinged by the darkening political scene.

Often, then, elements from sagas, fairy stories, detective novels, and psychology come in simply in their own right, as metaphors independent of the myth. *Which* are dependent and which independent is something only to be decided by critical examination, though the context normally gives a clear indication. A few stanzas from 'Danse Macabre' (1937), which treat religion ironically (God as 'Papa'), debunk the writer's pretensions as a leader in the fight against evil, anticipate war and death, and use fairy tale, biblical tale, and rude limerick to do so, may give some substance to this account.

The opening and the closing stanzas alone provide a sufficient context to suggest a serious general theme within the *content* of mythic frivolity and the popular ballad *form*. These bracketing stanzas go as follows:

> It's farewell to the drawing-room's mannerly cry,
> The professor's logical whereto and why,
> The frock-coated diplomat's polished aplomb,
> Now matters are settled with gas and with bomb.
> . . . .
> So good-bye to the house with its wallpaper red,
> Good-bye to the sheets on the warm double bed,
> Good-bye to the beautiful birds on the wall,
> It's good-bye, dear heart, good-bye to you all.
> (*Collected Poems*, ed. Mendelson, pp. 129 and 131)

The Spanish Civil War is nowhere mentioned directly, nor are Hitler and Mussolini or illegal German rearmamament – or the Freudian idea of repression by the individual's ego and superego, so that dangerous impulses become unconscious and therefore uncontrollable, volcanic, and perverse (devilish). Instead one gets the following fantasy which, if one knows the Auden myth, implies them all – and implies a relation between them (i.e. psychological causes of public catastrophe are implicitly taken to be more basic than economic ones):

> For the Devil has broken parole and arisen,
> He has dynamited his way out of prison,
> Out of the well where his Papa throws
> The rebel angel, the outcast rose.

Any suggestion of pompous egotism or arrogant do-goodery is negated by a sequence of humorously boastful stanzas, whose very extravagance suggests an inner conviction of futility and thus contributes to making the poem not absurd but moving by the time we come to the final stanza, already quoted. The sequence begins:

> For I, after all, am the Fortunate One,
> The Happy Go-Lucky, the spoilt Third Son;
> For me it is written the Devil to chase
> And to rid the world of the human race.

And it concludes:

> So Little John, Long John, Peter and Paul,
> And poor little Horace with only one ball,
> You shall leave your breakfast, your desk and your play
> On a fine summer morning the Devil to slay.

> For it's order and trumpet and anger and drum
> And power and glory command you to come;
> The graves will fly open to let you all in,
> And the earth be emptied of mortal sin.

(Op.cit.)

Since the fight against 'the Devil' seems likely to rid the world of the human race it is evident that Auden was already not uncritical of the communist war party, nor whole-heartedly in favour of psychological wholesomeness; both, it is implied, being less than 'human'.

On the other hand, 'The Wanderer' (1930) seems simply to use the idea of a compelling quest to symbolise a purely inward exploration, a personal test without any political implications. Whether Auden *intended* it to have them is unknowable and irrelevant. The point is that a narrative device (the Quest) that is sometimes used as a psycho-political (or, rarely, plain political) symbol is here found in a poem that gives no clues to such a use. References to 'borders' or 'guns' or 'class' or 'property' would probably have been enough to call up a shadowy outline of the wider myth, thus encouraging an interpretation of the quest as that *sort* of psychological effort needed to bring about political conviction and action. However, they are absent; so we need bring to the poem only knowledge of Auden's mythicising *habit* – to know, that is, that almost invariably in Auden setting and action are symbolical, not literal.

Orwell remarked of this period that:

> The whole left-wing ideology, scientific and utopian, was evolved by people who had no immediate prospect of attaining power.
>
> (Quoted by Buell, *W. H. Auden as a Social Poet*, p. 113)

There is a great deal of justice in this remark. Much left-wing literature is not responsible or constructive criticism, and no doubt that is a fault. The call to action in Auden, for instance, is usually so vague that it could just as well apply to fascism – as indeed could the exhortations to release the repressed material of the subconscious, especially when put in Lawrentian or Blakean terms. But this is a fact that Auden himself recognised, as he also recognised that sensible enquirers do not go to poetry for responsible social analysis and constructive criticism; they go to prose. The compensating advantage was that he could enliven the solemnity and ponderousness of Freud and Marx with a host of other cultural influences, most of which have been mentioned: sagas, fairy tales, spy stories, detective novels, film, popular song, opera, the Byron of *Don Juan* (witness *Letter to Lord Byron*), nonsense verse and light verse, the frivolous novels of Firbank and Wodehouse and the neurotic ones of Kafka. All these help to make his verse lively, stimulating, varied – and sometimes puzzling. It is rarely dull or pompous. More important, this variety enables it to engage with the actual complexity – of compound guilts, pacifism, and liberalism – beneath the overt Left/Right polarisation of the Thirties. The glimpse of this complexity of response already seen in the stanzas from 'Danse Macabre' is quite typical.

Perhaps more important than any of these influences, however, is that of Berlin, where Auden became familiar with the poetry of Brecht and the Brechtian notion of alienation – not allowing the reader to settle into the story or prevailing mood but instead forcing him to *consider* (at risk of boring him – hence the need for a lively surface). In Berlin, too, Auden came across political cabaret – popular song idiom adapted to social satire – and the cult of youth. All highly suited to his purposes in this period.

The American Period: Auden's Study of Kierkegaard

According to Peter Conrad, America was for Auden 'the Great Wrong Place', a place of trial and penitence, more appropriate than England for one who had come to believe that improvement must begin with the self, not society:

> Auden in America worships the austere Augustinian deity of Niebuhr, who has endowed men with the dangerous capacity for self-determination.
>
> (Conrad, *Imagining America*, p. 195)

Auden himself said that his emigration was a choice of perilous freedom, in a non-ideological country. Changing oneself, of course, is less exciting than changing society, so some of the exuberance goes out of Auden's verse; and being self-reliant is more lonely than being a Party member or fellow traveller. Much of this, however, suited Auden. He was accustomed to working by himself, with drawn curtains, his early bedtime forbade much participation in social or public cultural life anyway, and his favourite occupations were the solitary ones of reading, writing, listening to records of classical music, and solving difficult crossword puzzles. The dangerousness and unfriendliness of New York were in fact less penitential to him than they would have been to most exiles. The move had too the great advantage of freeing him from the burden of social responsibility, of being a leader of the intellectual left rather than simply a verbal artist. Besides, Auden adopted Kierkegaard's theological, rather than Sartre's atheistic existentialism; and there is one great comfort about theology: though it can't be proved right it can't be proved wrong. The course of history had led to disillusion with a secular doctrine but, given faith, no historical disaster *disproves* the belief in an inscrutable but good divine intention behind it.* Combine this comfort with the existentialist insistence on humanity's unique possession of individual consciousness and free-will, and you get a greater possibility of celebratory comedy than secular Marxism could offer, despites its doctrinal optimism.

In his 'Notes on the Comic' (*The Dyer's Hand*, 1963) Auden, like so many other writers on the subject makes the mistake of more or less equating comedy with what provokes laughter. Now, comedy does provoke laughter – but so does tickling, farce, and what we may call divertisement (or intellectual farce). The equation, then, is of little use for literary criticism, which is a discriminatory craft. On Auden's definition comedy would run throughout his work; but in the English period the laughter is usually for amusement only; it evades rather than conveys underlying seriousness, or is self-protective. Therefore it tends to come within the orbit of farce or divertisement (laughter for its own sake) as against comedy, usefully distinguished as significant laughter (laughter for the sake of something else).

Comedy is less hilarious than farce (the audience must be sufficiently detached to perceive the point); that is why it suits a detached poet like Auden. That so much of his later work should be comedy, and what's more *celebratory* comedy, however, is paradoxical, for the Kierkegaardian philosophy he adopted led Kierkegaard himself into

*e.g.   . . . As we bury our dead
    We know without knowing there is reason for what we bear.
                    ('Memorial for a City', *Collected Poems*, ed. Mendelson, p. 451)

W. H. Auden in 1953, photographed by Sir Cecil Beaton

the deepest gloom – and indeed *angst*, anxiety or dread, is taken to be a necessary concomitant to existentialism.

By definition, Kierkegaard argued, the divine is infinitely removed from the human, therefore, though man must obey God's will, he cannot know what *is* God's will. He must act in blind faith. One good reason for *angst*. Another good reason inheres in man's absolute freedom and duty to choose. He cannot blame what he is or does on either heredity or environment; he is responsible for himself, and he *must* choose in order to be fully human – but he may choose wrongly, and cannot know whether he has done so or not, for his choice is not to be judged by its social results but by its correspondence to the divine will. A third reason for *angst* is that a proper faith cannot be arrived at on satisfactory human grounds, for it can be demonstrated that Christianity is neither moral (because of the necessity of obedience), nor rational (because of its commitment to the unknowable), nor socially beneficial (witness the historical record). Faith, then, must be arrived at by 'a leap in the dark'. What will persuade men to take such a leap? Worldly disasters. Logically, then, reform and improvement are hardly to be welcomed, though they may be desired. Another cause for *angst*. On the other hand, it means one doesn't need to bother; that whatever one does may be wrong, so one can do as one likes (provided it is done in the faith that it is what God commands). Auden puts it this way:

> The command of God is 'Choose to do what at this moment in this context I am telling you to do'.
>> (Introduction to *The Living Thoughts of Kierkegaard*, 1952.
>> *Forewords and Afterwords*, ed. Mendelson, p. 177)

Hardly logical, but it fits well with the existentialist emphasis on the moment, the obligation of constant free choice, and tends to cancel out the implications of other aspects of the doctrine – summed up by Auden as follows:

> To show the non-believer that he is in despair because he cannot believe in *his* gods and then show him that Christ cannot be a man-made God because in every way he is offensive to the natural man is for Kierkegaard the only true apologetics.
>> (Ibid. p. 180)

For someone whose commitment is intellectual rather than emotional, someone always inclined anyway to see things in a long perspective and with some irony or frivolity, there is as much reason, then, for serene human comedy as for despair – and indeed both can go together: the self-made misery, the self-destruction, of the species that considers itself the highest of the animals (and a rational one, to boot) *is* wryly comic – if one can stand far enough back to see it so.

Other aspects of existentialism are harder to reconcile with Auden's actual poetic practice. In fact they seem flatly contradictory to it – though as existentialism itself is not an entirely consistent system the differences may not be as blatant as they seem. The truth is that existentialism is not really a philosophy at all but a psychology, and as such appealed to Auden. It does not inquire into the truth of concepts but into the nature of man. And it makes statements more than it argues logically; so there is no great difficulty in taking from it what seems useful and ignoring it when it appears at odds with human experience. If 'truth' is not logical truth but lived truth, as Kierkegaard maintains, and if human being is in fact *becoming*, then truth must be changeable, indeed constantly changing. Hence its near-fusion with the obligations of 'authenticity' and constant choice. An idea with some very odd consequences, logical and practical, but at least one that leaves a poet with opportunities for scope and variety.

One thing that no doubt attracted Auden to Kierkegaard was his emphasis on the individual – a great change from Marx. But there is a sense in which his particular kind of emphasis is unsuitable for literature. Though he attacked Hegel, the arch-idealist, for making an abstract Absolute the focus of reality, he himself shares much with idealism. The basic premise of idealism is that reality is dependent on, or determined by experience. Taken to a logical extreme, this premise gives rise to many awkward questions. Does the world momentarily cease to exist every time we blink? Do British trains – as G. E. Moore asked – not have wheels while they are in the station? Following Kant's view that we see the world not as it really is but through our own spectacles of space and time, it is argued, less extremely, that we *know* only our own experience: *that* is our world. A scientist might counter this by suggesting that we have evolved those particular spectacles because they enable us to see the world the way it really is and thus to survive in it. An objective philosopher might argue that to have a sensation is already to have passed out of the circle of the self, and indeed there seems plenty of evidence to show that sensations come and go and correspond to an external reality. Kierkegaard, however, was a subjective philosopher who detested scientists and all objective rationality. Auden's summary of Kierkegaard (op.cit.), which he clearly approves, goes something like this:

a) each person holds with absolute certainty the belief that he exists, but this is a private and incommunicable belief – and anyone else's existence cannot become an object of knowledge;

b) one's knowledge does include, however, an awareness of a freedom to make choices – but the act of choice cannot be objectively observed (or it would not be a real *choice*);

c) it also includes an awareness of time as an eternal present; and

d) we necessarily live in a state of anxiety or dread, pride, despair or faith (all allegedly unobservable; simply *lived*).

The view that the only reality with which men should have to do (the only one really knowable) is that of their own conscious existence, would make poetry, and indeed all other utterances, almost pointless. Auden in fact writes about people, events and the world as if they were real and really knowable. The view that anyone else's existence cannot become an object of knowledge, should lead to callousness (as should the belief that suffering is needed to promote the 'leap in the dark' to faith). Auden in fact writes with great compassion and shows no relish for either personal or social disaster. Choice, however, does seem to be relished – and is often enough a choice of the pleasurable. The belief in the inescapability of *angst* in the human condition, does give much of his poetry a certain shadow and sadness, but does not prevent it from being comedy, in the strict sense, even celebratory comedy. His poem on the senses, 'Precious Five' (*Collected Poems*, ed. Mendelson, p. 447) concludes:

> Be happy, precious five,
> So long as I'm alive
> . . . .
> I could (which you cannot)
> Find reasons fast enough
> To face the sky and roar
> In anger and despair . . .

But the sky would merely command:

> *Bless what there is for being*

The awareness of time as an eternal present seems to be partially accepted in practice by Auden in so far as he commonly collapses ancient and modern periods, or legendary and real histories – but in order to suggest that there is an essential human condition rather than to deny the reality of the past.

Kierkegaard's influence, then, is by no means as complete as Auden's own statements would lead one to expect. This is not really surprising, however, for several reasons. Firstly, Kierkegaard believed that man should transcend, first, the aesthetic state, then the ethical, to rest finally in the religious. A doctrine inimical to even a religious poet, for all poetry needs body; and Auden's later poetry (after the long poems of his conversion years) is almost entirely aesthetic and ethical rather than religious. Secondly, Kierkegaard in spite of being passionately Christian (or perhaps because of it) hated and despised the established Churches: Auden was a practising member of a High Church establishment. Thirdly, where Kierkegaard is urgent, Auden is humorously contemplative. Finally, and most importantly, though Auden *theoretically* accepts as a reason for the artistic vocation's now being more difficult than in the past a 'loss of belief in the significance and reality of sensory phenomena', his *poetry* emphasises the objective reality of nature. True, he seems to take from Kierkegaard the idea of its 'otherness' (an idea shared also with Sartre), but does not go on to assert its unknowableness or to suggest that either it, or our perceptions of it, are illusory. Witness the following examples:

> The eyes of the crow and the eye of the camera open
> Onto Homer's world, not ours. First and last
> They magnify earth, the abiding
> Mother of gods and men . . .
> . . . .
> She alone is seriously there.
> ('Memorial for a City', *Collected Poems*, ed. Mendelson, p. 450)

Of course, Auden is going on to assert that there is a higher Reality accessible only to man, but he is far from denying the objective validity of that of the crow and the camera, or of Homer.

> All that which lies outside our sort of why,
> Those wordless creatures who are there as well,
> Remote from mourning yet in sight and cry,
> Make time more golden than we meant to tell.
>
> ('Objects', Op.cit., p. 473)

'. . . than we meant to tell' seems to record a little guilt at this aesthetic appreciation of independently existing, godless animals, but it is certainly expressed by the poem. Or take this:

> So large a morning *so itself* to lean
> Over so many and such little hills
> All at rest in roundness and rigs of green
>
> ('The Song', Op.cit. p. 474. Italics added)

That the world is not merely a creation of our subjective perception seems to be stressed. And surely Auden is being positively contradictory of Kierkegaard when he writes: 'Thousands have lived without love, not one without water' ('First Things First'). To conclude, one complete little poem that illustrates several of the points made, and incidentally exemplifies many of the virtues of Auden's remarkable nature poetry, which will require consideration in Part Two:

> A shot: from crag to crag
>   The tell-tale echoes trundle;
> Some feathered he-or-she
>   Is now a lifeless bundle
> And, proud into a kitchen, some
> Example of our tribe will come.
>
> Down in the startled valley
>   Two lovers break apart:
> He hears the roaring oven
>   Of a witch's heart;
> Behind his murmurs of her name
> She sees a marksman taking aim.
>
> Reminded of the hour
>   And that his chair is hard,
> A deathless verse half done,
>   One interrupted bard
> Postpones his dying with a dish
> Of several suffocated fish.
>
> ('Hunting Season', Op.cit., p. 420)

A good many things could be said about this unpretentious poem – its unpretentiousness being one of them. There is the ease of it, the way rhyme and metre blend effortlessly with clear sense and normal syntax; the economy: each stanza has the shot at its heart; the range, from the practical world to the artistic, the physical to the psychological; the subtle use of fairy-story; the sardonic overtones of 'proud', 'example' and 'deathless'; and the implications of remaining savagery in 'tribe'. But what is chiefly relevant here is the evidence of humane feelings despite an inhumane philosophy, and the clear assumption of the full reality of others, even animals. And finally, the evidence that Auden is far more than, and different from, the sum of his influences, whether biographical, political or cultural.

Part Two
Critical Survey

4 General

The Hawk and the Crow

'My poetry doesn't change from place to place', Auden is reported to have said, 'it changes with the years.' Something of those changes – together with underlying samenesses – has already been noted. A closer look at two passages used earlier in different contexts may serve to foreground their literary-critical relevance:

> Consider this and in our time
> As the hawk sees it or the helmeted airman:
> The clouds rift suddenly – look there
> At cigarette-end smouldering on a border
> At the first garden party of the year.
> Pass on, admire the view of the massif
> Through plate-glass windows of the Sport Hotel;
> Join there the insufficient units
> Dangerous, easy, in furs, in uniform
> And constellated at reserved tables
> Supplied with feelings by an efficient band
> Relayed elsewhere to farmers and their dogs
> Sitting in kitchens in the stormy fens.   (1930)
> > (*Collected Poems*, ed. Mendelson, p. 61)

> The eyes of the crow and the eye of the camera open
> Onto Homer's world, not ours. First and last
> They magnify earth, the abiding
> Mother of gods and men; if they notice either
> It is only in passing: gods behave, men die,
> Both feel in their own small way, but She
> does nothing and does not care.
> She alone is seriously there.   (1949)
> > (Ibid. p. 450)

Both passages take a long view. In that they are similar. They differ in the kind of view; in the one case physical, in the other philosophical. Both contrast man and nature, and find man insignificant and impermanent by comparison. But whereas this is stated in the second example, it is only implied in the first; the first is more dramatic, the second more reflective. Furthermore, nature seems menacing in the first, merely indifferent in the second passage. And in the second case what is said applies to all men equally (and to gods), while the first passage seems to distinguish somewhat between the nobs behind plate-

Spender, Auden, Hughes, Eliot and MacNeice at a Faber party in 1961

glass and the farmers who are at home with the menace. Again, both passages are in free verse, or fairly free verse. But oddly, the first seems to be more modernistic although in fact it is more regularly stressed than the second. Before going on to examine the reasons for this interesting and significant impression, it is relevant to say that 'Consider' goes off badly after this first paragraph, and remains a much less consistent poem than 'Memorial for a City' despite revision of the latter part by Auden; a fairly typical difference between early and later work.

That the first passage only *seems* more modernistic is not to be accounted for merely because it is relatively regularly stressed. The fact is that Auden had little in common with either modernism or the avant-garde to begin with, and that little became less as he went on:

> Re-reading my poems, I find that in the nineteen-thirties I fell into some very slovenly verbal habits. The definite article is always a headache to any poet writing in English, but my addiction to German usages became a disease. Again, it makes me wince when I see how ready I was to treat -*or* and -*aw* as homophones. It is true that in the Oxonian dialect I speak they are, but that isn't really an adequate excuse. I also find that my ear will not longer tolerate rhyming a voiced *S* with an unvoiced. (1965)
>
> (Quoted in *Collected Poems*, ed. Mendelson, p. 16)

An eighteenth-century care for correctness, for setting a good example, rather than the linguistic iconoclasm typical of post-romantic modernism or avant-gardism.

Modernists, led by Eliot and Pound tended to be reactionary, religious, and subjective. They fragmented language and abrogated coherent sense in order to create an expressive form that would model their own sense of internal fracture. They believed the poem to be an autonomous aesthetic entity, neither intended nor able to heal the poet or the modern society in which he felt so little at home. Auden on the other hand, in the Thirties, was radical, not reactionary, in his opinions, atheistic not religious, and detached not subjective; he thought of himself as a healer, and did believe that words could affect beliefs and therefore action. By the time he had become liberal and religious, he had become even less subjective and less inclined to maltreat the English language (save in one respect, to be examined later). The influence of Hopkins, shared with the modernists, drops away, and with it the Anglo-Saxon contortions that produce much of the early obscurity (later obscurity is a matter of content more than form). Avant-gardism – dada, surrealism, shape-poetry – is characterised by iconoclasm and the pursuit of novelty. Auden was in principle *constructively* radical or liberal, and, far from striving for novelty for novelty's sake, looked back in the traditional way for useful models: Horace, Icelandic sagas, Dante, Goethe, Pope, Byron, Hardy. Moreover, unlike both modernists and avant-gardists, he thought poetry both could and should provoke thought (amongst other things).

So, the reader is urged to 'Consider' – and 'in our time', for the writer is at home in his age, unlike Eliot and Pound, though he may not like it; and he does think something can be done about it – after rational thought has been applied to political and personal sickness, neurotic or economic, physical or mental. A sense of urgency is generated by further imperatives, 'look', 'pass on', 'admire', 'join'. The reader is not encouraged to indulge in passive appreciation. But one of the merits of the Thirties' poetry is that at its best it does manage the remarkable feat of combining aesthetic pleasure (which requires a certain detachment) with a sense of busy stirring up and urging on. In

65

this case, the urgency of the imperative 'consider' is moderated both by the meaning (ponder, think about) and the removed viewpoint ('As the hawk sees it or the helmeted airman'); so that we are well able at one and the same time to *respond* to the idea of imminent danger and to *appreciate* the way in which it is conveyed.

The hawk and the helmeted airman are related subliminally by the alliteration, and that in turn hints at a common menace, for the hawk is a bird of prey, not simply admiring the scenery. The hint is picked up immediately, in lines reminiscent of film technique. Suddenly we pierce the cloud that befogs us and see – what? In long-shot a political border (which in Auden may also signify a psychological one), for it would be impossible from that height to see a garden border. But the long-shot fades into a close-up. We see not only a garden border (supported by 'garden party') but even a cigarette-end smouldering on it. Do cigarette-ends smoulder? Possibly, but more typically, fuses and anger smoulder while cigarette-ends glow or burn – and thus the political *and* psychological implications of 'border' are kept in mind. The smart set implied by the 'first' garden party (of many) is itself on a border, literally between seasons ('first') and metaphorically between peace and war, civilisation and destruction ('airman', 'smoulder'). We cut then to another bourgeois group, presumably at a winter-sports resort, admiring from their comfortable shelter a looming massif that makes plate-glass protection seem fragile. In the political context 'units' suggests army groups – 'insufficient' to deal with the forces gathering against them (in turn vaguely associated with the natural forces symbolised by the massif and the stormy fens). They are also insufficient because they are single units each for himself, rather than a coherent social body believing in 'each for all and all for each', a separateness implied by the scattered stars of 'constellated', and the pun in 'reserved'. In the psychological context, they are insufficient* as human beings (hence the need to be 'supplied with feelings'). Though dangerous they are doomed, since it is clear that the tough toilers (the 'farmers') associated with the vast forces of nature (comparable perhaps to Marx's forces of history) are not defeatable.

This passage, then, is densely packed and dramatic – even a little melodramatic – and, though clearer than much of the early work, sufficiently imprecise to allow readers some liberty of interpretation. For instance, one doesn't have to associate the forces of nature with those of history, but it is not outright ridiculous to do so: and the 'insufficient units' could reasonably be fascists, or fascist sympathisers, or just capitalist drones, according to taste. So it is easy to understand why it should have been widely felt that Auden deteriorated after the Thirties.

*Note the ironic internal rhyme with 'efficient'.

The second passage, opening 'Memorial to a City', lacks the excitement of the first, and its meaning is complex rather then dense. That is to say, it does not lie in ambiguities (like those of 'smoulder' or 'units') but in ideas. Why should doing nothing and not caring alone qualify for being 'seriously there'? Why does Auden go on to say:

> The steady eyes of the crow and the camera's candid eye
> See as honestly as they know how, but they lie.
> The crime of life is not time.

Moreover, despite the rather looser verse-form, no one could take this as modernist or avant-garde writing. It is clearly not trying to be up-to-date, or selfconsciously rejecting poetry of the past (though it is not imitating it either). In any case it is too lucid and contemplative, in an intellectual way, for such writing.

There is, however, much to say on the other side. Instead of the visual filmic mode – a little flip perhaps? – we have a brooding meditative one. This has certainly gone out of fashion since modernism emerged from the chrysalis of imagism, but it is at least arguable that commentary is the more suitable task for words; purveying significant images, for films or paintings. Whether the more relaxed unbuttoned style is better or worse is a matter of opinion. All one can say for sure is that the civilised manner, of serious conversation, has its own different attraction. On closer inspection, too, more is to be found in this verse than at first appears.

That the eyes of the crow open onto Homer's world seems evident enough. Crows have no part in our post-industrial civilisation – they are part of a more primitive world. But Auden's main point is to do with value-free vision, and that is why the eye of the camera is needed too. It makes the point that the bird is a sort of machine. For both, as for Homer, facts are facts, events events, and once they have occurred they are irredeemable. There is a delicate literary frisson in seeing that in this sense the post-Homeric camera does open onto Homer's world, and an even more delicate one in seeing that it does not open on to ours. That is if we go along for the moment with Auden's premise that the essential difference between the two worlds is not that one is pre-industrial and the other post-industrial, but that they are pre- and post-Christian respectively. 'Open', too, though not immediately striking like some of the diction of 'Consider', does more than merely state the prose fact that a shutter is moved from a lens. Literally, of course, neither the crow nor the camera sees Homer's world. In common usage windows 'open' onto scenes larger and brighter than the room, narrow defiles 'open' onto lighter and larger landscapes – and 'open' comes at the end of a line, followed by a pause and a white space. Hence the underlying suggestion of a sudden vision, of a more sunlit, spacious world than ours: a suggestion confirmed by the 'barbed-wire' scenes the crow and the camera are said to record, in the next paragraph. Homer's world, whose values were all of this earth, is thus presented so fairly that there is again a frisson of surprise when we come to find that it is being argued *against*, in favour of the mixture of guilt, despair, and hope of redemption in the Christian world. 'First and last' reminds us of the Christian first and last things, which are not worldly – and thus gives a pejorative overtone to 'magnify'. This cannot be literal, and therefore must mean 'overemphasise'.

Yet we are told that 'She alone is seriously there'. How can that be? Well, she *is* abiding, does give birth to gods and men and will still be gravely there when they and their spoliations, pettiness, and frivolities have passed away (presumably Auden excludes the Christian god from this genesis and this fate). She cannot help being authentic for 'She/Does nothing and does not care'; she just unpretendingly *is*, and is the basis for everything else in nature. But this is rather a negative form of seriousness or sincerity of being. And this is the turning-point of Auden's case, for we can hardly help siding with those gods and men, who 'feel', in however small a way, as against a seriousness, unfrivolous, authentic, and faithfully mothering though it may be, that is wholly neutral. This is what makes the epigrammatic paradox of 'See as *honestly* as they know how, but they lie' meaningful and not merely smart. Why do they lie? Because they miss the main truth that as events in time are redeemable outside, or apart from time, time as not the crime of life. They see only facts, not values; whereas our grief at the horrors of life 'is not Greek: As we bury our dead/We know without knowing there is reason for what we bear'.

We need accept neither Auden's political, nor his theological views to get a good deal of pleasure and profit from both these passages. After all, if poetry lifts or enlivens the heart, mind, or spirits, it is as much by reason of *how* it says as by *what* it says. In these cases, we are treated, respectively, to the pleasures of multiple viewpoints, suggestive juxtapositions, and intellectually stimulating ambiguities; and to the pleasures of paradox, metaphysical range, the stimulation of being lifted out of the confines of the present and everyday, together with an aesthetic combination of conversational ease and economy of expression.

In addition, of course, the novelty of utterance, in each case, does make us *consider* certain points, either for the first time or afresh. And though we may not be convinced of the basic beliefs they derive from, we may well find the point worthy of consideration. After all, man *is* trivial and impermanent by comparison with the earth that has given birth to him and will outlast him. A point we need to be pricked by as we do our damnedest to ruin that world, perhaps to unleash lethal forces as we do so. Furthermore, there is no harm is being reminded that individuals may well feel some parallels between natural, and historical forces that can so soon become overwhelming and unstoppable. It seems also true that the way in which man seems to transcend nature, as a massif or a crow do not, though it has not led to any indisputable increase in happiness or merit, does seem somehow worthwhile. Who would choose to be a crow? That one doesn't have to choose to be a Christian in order to reject crowdom, or a communist to reject fascism, may reduce the impact of these poems a little – but not very much. The qualities of expression, the stimulation, the provocativeness, and sometimes the validity of the points implied remain, no matter what the originating belief.

'Poem in October' and 'Aubade'

Two further quotations may give more precision to our idea of what is characteristic of Auden, the Audenesque quality that unmistakably distinguishes work of either period as his and no-one else's. The first is the opening stanza of Dylan Thomas's 'Poem in October', the second that of Auden's 'Aubade'. Each, the better to illustrate the point, is a fairly extreme example of the author's manner:

> It was my thirtieth year to heaven
> Woke to my hearing from harbour and neighbour wood
> And the mussel pooled and the heron
>   Priested shore
>   The morning beckon
> With water spraying and the call of seagull and rook
> And the knock of sailing boats on the net webbed wall
>   Myself to set foot
>   That second
>   In the still sleeping town and set forth.

> Beckoned anew to a World
> where wishes alter nothing,
> expelled from the padded cell
> of Sleep and re-admitted
> to involved Humanity,
> again, as wrote Augustine,
> I know what I am and will,
> I am willing and knowing,
> I will to be and to know,
> facing in four directions,
> outwards and inwards in Space,
> observing and reflecting,
> backwards and forwards through Time,
> recalling and forecasting.
>   (*Collected Poems*, ed. Mendelson, p. 658)

Both stanzas deal with the same subject: waking up and being beckoned into the daytime world. Both are good of their kind. But how different the kinds are! Thomas's verse is almost entirely expressive (of personal sensuous feeling), Auden's almost entirely reflective (on the general case of which his is a typical instance). Auden's diction is conceptual, Thomas's perceptual. If feeling-states arise from reading the Auden piece they do so as a shadow cast by the brilliance of the thought and the concentrated lucidity of the style. If ideas arise from the Thomas piece they are merely shadows resulting from our apprehension of the significance of the set of perceptions expressed. Despite his elaborate stanza-form, Thomas appears, and is, the more modernist – and therefore, although Auden is much clearer, there is a sense in which it is Auden who requires more explanation. For, since the Romantics reacted against the expository, public poetry of the eighteenth century, there has been a tacit assumption that such work is 'not poetry'. The answer to this seems to be that if we are to persist in the profitless habit of taking 'poetry' as a value-loaded term rather than a neutral word for works in verse, then conceptual verse is something else just as interesting in its different way.

Apart from the merely idiosyncratic omission of hyphens, probably the first thing that strikes us about the Thomas stanza is the lack of punctuation and grammar. Nor is the one the cause of the other; no amount of punctuation could turn this into a grammatical statement. But grammar is a way of clarifying utterances by putting them into orderly perspectives of time, mood, and subordination; it is also public, an agreed system that enables members of a speech-community to communicate with minimal difficulty. Thomas, however, wishes to convey a *private* experience, and one, moreover, that is instantaneous. The last thing he wants is clarity, for here we have the poet waking on the morning of what is generally regarded as the most significant of birthdays, and feeling the world rush in through all the appropriate senses. This has to be evoked (inevitably within time – the time it takes to get from 'It' to 'forth') together with the instantaneously accompanying mood. Hence the lack of punctuation and grammar, so that everything *seems* to merge with everything else. In particular we may note that though 'the morning beckons' is possible English grammar, as is 'the morning beacon', 'the morning beckon' is not. So we get the impression of being at once beckoned forth by the sounds of morning, by a pantheistic religious feeling for nature ('heron priested', 'water praying'), and by the beacon of the morning light. Perhaps the 'beacon', too, adds a sense of adventure, a call to a quest: to set forth *that second!* Only the stanza-form preserves us from chaos. After all, Thomas is rightly creating an objective correlative for the inner experience he wishes to express; and though not an orderly experience it is not an experience of chaos *as such*; rather it is a sort of multiple vision. In line-length the form goes in and out like a concertina – in marked contrast to the metronomic orderliness of the Auden piece – a movement appropriate to the alternating

moods the poem goes on to record. And the assonances and consonances that substitute for regular rhyme (heaven/heron, wood/rook,
beckon/second, foot/forth) also tactfully diminish the sense of our
tendency to order experience. So the impression of spontaneous
perceptions, captured as it were on the wing, remains the dominant
one.

Almost everything in the Auden stanza is at the opposite end of the
stylistic spectrum. The lines are regular, the punctuation very careful
indeed, the grammar perfectly correct, the thought clear, cogent, and
progressive. There is no reference to a particular morning or place, or
to physical objects, or to the senses of sound, sight, texture, or muscular
tension as in the Thomas stanza. World, Sleep, Humanity, Space, and
Time are given capital letters, not to personify them, but to indicate
that we are dealing with general entities; they correct any implication
of particularity in the use of 'I'.

Far from aiming at immediacy and involvement, Auden is disengag-
ing himself and the reader from such things and is aiming for
philosophic detachment; he is concerned not with the feeling of his
subject matter but its significance in relation to the nature of the world
and the self. Though metaphysical in its concerns, the stanza eschews
jargon (not, alas, a notable virtue of his Germanic sources). That this
too is in some sort one experience, or one web of related thought, is
indicated by its being a single sentence. But it is marvellously
managed, so that if we pay attention to the punctuation all the
relationships are made clear, the points are seen to be logically
progressive; and the various balances (of knowing and willing, of
facing, of observing, reflecting, recalling and forecasting) emphasise
precisely what Thomas minimises, the structuring effort we make,
physically and mentally, to preserve our harmonious tension with
reality. The clarity is combined with an economy that yields its own
kind of aesthetic pleasure. 'Again', for instance, carefully cradled
between commas, indicates not only the regularity of readmittance to
Humanity, but more specifically the fact that this habitually entails
both a sense of selfhood and of willing and of knowing, and indeed that
all these are part of a necessary structuring process. By implication,
nothing of this is characteristic of the world of Sleep – nor is it
necessary there, for that is not a real world and there are no real
penalties for absurd behaviour. As 'padded cell' implies, it is a lunatic
world where Space and Time are merely imaginary and the dreamer is
its creator. 'Involved' surely suggests not only the complexity of the
real world and of the human personality (which necessitate the
structuring effort noted) but also that people are there involved with
each other. The dreamer can safely be a loner; waking, this would be
dangerous to oneself and others. So the poem indirectly implies a need
for social responsibility and links it with personal complex creative
structuring.

This stanza is not quite so abstract as it seems. 'Facing in four directions' is unobtrusively metaphorical, for instance. Literally, we face only in one direction, forwards in space. 'Expelled' seems to hint at birth – into a world from which one must separate oneself, become unthinglike, in order to manage and be human. After all, dangerous lunatics are not *expelled* from padded cells; presumably they don't want to stay there. And, of course, antithesis, parallelism, and chiasmus, as we have indicated, act here as formal metaphor.

Nevertheless, though this stanza illustrates a distinguishing tendency in Auden, it is not average or typical. Most of his work is more metaphorical, much of it more lyrical (though, in keeping with the tendency illustrated, meditatively so); some is dramatic, some narrative, some popular in form and content, some elaborate in form and erudite or esoteric in content.

Problems and Difficulties

This range can be formalised somewhat as follows (going from a work's most general aspect, *Mode*, to its most particular, *Form*): in *Mode*, the poetry is fictional, didactic, metaphoric, comic, contemplative, argumentative, or fantastic; in *Type*, dramatic, narrative, or lyric; in *Kind*, allegory, myth, parable, epigram, song, play, or meditation. The *Form* may be that of free verse, metre, rhyme, half-rhyme, or syllabics. Everything is to be found in both periods, though the fantastic mode diminishes in the American period and the argumentative and the comic increase, while the dramatic tends to be embodied in opera libretti and rather formal dialogues instead of in plays. Furthermore, poems may exemplify any mixture of modes, types, kinds and forms. For critical purposes, Auden is difficult to categorise usefully.

For that reason it seems better to start a critical assessment of his work by discussion, not of categories, but of the difficulties it may present to the reader; and then go on to the rewards it offers. At first sight, perhaps a surprising approach to a poet who was in principle public not private, wished his work to entertain or instruct (or both), who did believe in the value of a paraphrasable content of ideas and did not believe in novelty of form for novelty's sake, and who often used simple popular forms, as in such ballads as 'Victor' or 'Miss Gee' and jazz-songs like 'Refugee Blues'. For such a poet, why should clearing away difficulties take a high priority? Most of Auden's own statements about poetry, too, seem to point away from the obscurity and esotericism characteristic of much modernist work:

> We can only ...
> look at
> this world with a happy eye
> but from a sober perspective
> ('The Horatians', *Collected Poems*, ed. Mendelson, p. 581)

> Blessed be all metrical rules that forbid automatic responses,
> force us to have second thoughts, free from the fetters of Self.
>
> No, Surrealists, no! No, even the wildest of poems
> must, like prose, have a firm basis in staid commonsense.
>
> I suspect that without some undertone of the comic
> genuine serious verse cannot be written today.
>
> > ('Shorts II', Ibid. pp. 642–3)

Indeed, what could be clearer, seen with happier eye – though from a sober perspective – metrically more distancing, more common-sensical, or seriously witty, than, say, 'The Willow-wren and the Stare'?

Much the same could be said of many of the early poems, and of the whole of the 'Letter to Lord Byron', though few perhaps skate along the edge of disaster with such masterly poise as 'The Willow-wren and the Stare'. Unhappily, the same also *cannot* be said of many poems in both periods, though it is probably true to say that the Thirties' work presents a higher proportion of problems.

Other things being equal, of course, it is proper to prefer a clear poem to an obscure one. Unfortunately, other things rarely are equal – not often enough, at any rate, for it to be possible simply to ignore the more obscure poems on the grounds that the others are better anyway; for sometimes poems are clear because they are crude, obscure because they are complex; sometimes a worthwhile originality of style exacts no more than a reasonable price in terms of difficulty, or simply a poem will be obscure in the absence of a gloss on its references to certain fields of information or ideas.

Such difficulties, however, are by no means the only ones to be added to those inherent in what must be considered Auden's most persistent concern throughout his career: 'the baffle of being'. This is a major source of his comedy (often mediated stylistically by incongruous juxtapositions of different linguistic registers: witness, say, *lamb*/*lascivious*, *joy*/*goody*, in 'The Willow-wren and the Stare'); it is also a major source of both complexity and confusion.

Marx and Kierkegaard would have agreed – for they share in the Hegelian tradition, however they amend it – that man is in an absurd situation, which he cannot get out of unless he submits himself to a larger force – and then not in his lifetime; they agree further, that worldly 'truth' is practical, a matter of the engagement of an authentic self with the environment. In essence, though both would have put it differently (and less well), they would have found little to disagree with in Pope's formulation, which admirably indicates why the human situation, so viewed, should promote comedy, complexity, or confusion (or all three):

> Plac'd on this isthmus of a middle state,
> A being darkly wise and rudely great:

With too much knowledge for the sceptic side,
With too much weakness for the stoic's pride,
He hangs between; in doubt to act, or rest;
In doubt to deem himself a god, or beast;
In doubt his mind or body to prefer;
Born but to die, and reas'ning but to err;
Alike in ignorance, his reason such,
Whether he thinks too little or too much:
Chaos of thought and passion, all confus'd;
Still by himself abus'd or disabus'd;
Created half to rise, and half to fall;
Great lord of all things, yet a prey to all;
Sole judge of truth, in endless error hurl'd:
The glory, jest, and riddle of the world!

(from the *Essay on Man*)

Freud's doctrines, too, are perfectly compatible with:

Chaos of thought and passion, all confus'd;
Still by himself abus'd or disabus'd.

If Auden tends to emphasise the jest more than the glory, there is nevertheless a constant feeling that the riddle of man in nature and society is worth teasing out.

If the baffle of being or, to put it another way, the matter of integration, is one's chief concern, difficulties are naturally to be expected; for concern implies a problem – a problem with more than one aspect, since it results from disintegratedness. In the Thirties both Marx's idea, of dialectical forces operating in society and alienating forces in man, and Freud's idea, that everything could have an unconscious feeling or motive at odds with the apparent one, impelled Auden away from simplicity. Later, he derived from Kierkegaard the idea that life is characterised by irreconcilable categories, especially those of the body and the spirit, the Here-and-Now and the Wholly Other. The easy way to deal with such contraries, of course, is that of the romantic expressionist poet like Thomas: simply to accept and reflect them, to throw oneself into this sea of troubles and make a splash. Auden prefers to take arms against it, so to speak, to subsume it in a broader synthesis in the Marxian way, or control it by making it fully conscious as Freud argued, or dominate it by a free act of will as Kierkegaard ordered. Ronald Carter sums up this point well:

Auden is not a poet of minute particulars, nor one who enters fully and reciprocally into his subjects, tending instead towards the general, even multiple perspective .... Rather than a withdrawal from experience or a retreat from the exigencies of self into a series of protective personae, this represents ... more Auden's indirect yet playfully personal way of saying that, as far as the subject of the poetry goes, all depends on how we look at it . . . . His purpose is not to have it all ways but to suggest that the process of seeing is a complex one.

(W. H. Auden 'City Without Walls', *Agenda* ed. Cookson)

In the earlier period particularly, it is often difficult to distinguish complexity from confusion. Sometimes, for instance, Auden adopts the persona of a bourgeois whose own utterances unwittingly give him away, the reader, then, being supposed to blame the ostensible hero and approve his enemy. For such a method to work a clear and controlled style is necessary. But in the early Thirties especially, Auden often adopted an elliptic Anglo-Saxon manner that can easily become unclear in an uninflected language like modern English in which clarity of meaning depends on word-order:

> In legend all were simple,
> And held the straitened spot;
> But we in legend not,
> Are not simple.

('The Bonfires', *Collected Poems*, ed. Mendelson, p. 53)

Awkward, but reasonably clear; a line like 'Before born and is still mother' is cryptic as a rendering of the plain English statement 'and /*the child*/ is still the mother before being born'. Again – especially in the earlier period – Auden's use of myth and symbolism can be troublesome, for both tend to be seen with double vision. Thus, the saga-hero is admired for his indomitable courage but is recognised to represent the crude values of a gangster, or public-school, society. The spies or agents in one of Auden's modern-myth poems may be genuinely engaged on an heroic quest to attain personal and/or social integration, to pass over a symbolic border or break through a barrier, or they may be representing the Truly Weak Man who *thinks* he is a Truly Strong Man but is self-deceiving. The Truly Strong Man can afford not to prove himself. Or again, nonsense, fantasy, or dream-logic may be used to indicate either that the persona is a neurotic (witness the paranoic voice of 'There Will be No Peace') or that the poem is to be taken allegorically – or, it often appears, both: Auden hasn't made up his mind. Sometimes too (in both periods) the same symbol may symbolise different things in different poems (or even the same poem); the mother may be a life-giving undulant mammary landscape or the Enemy, Dragon or Giantess.

Because Auden's landscapes are always symbolic – usually psychologically symbolic in the Thirties, morally so thereafter – the reader is tempted to assume that they are always Freudian or Kierkegaardian. Thus, the title of 'Paysage Moralisé' (Moralised Landscape) tells us that this is not a descriptive nature poem; so John Fuller, in his heroic *Reader's Guide*, says that the mountains are phallic, the valleys uterine. It is true that the poem was written in 1933, when Auden may well have intended this to be so – in places. Hardly throughout though; for what then would we make of 'the green trees blossomed on the mountains', for instance – gangrene of the penis? And as for 'moping villages in valleys' . . . the mind boggles! If Auden was using Freud at all, it has to be said that he was doing so very optimistically, and must take the incongruous consequences. Since the writing does not at all *point to* a Freudian interpretation, one ought to say that whatever he may be supposed to have meant, on grounds of period, the poem in fact is symbolical in a different way.

Again, Auden tends to use paradox, or riddling phrases, as a kind of formal image of the complicated contrariety of the 'baffle of being' – often seen dualistically in terms of body/spirit (symbolically sea/desert), necessity/freedom, actuality/wishing, time/eternity, reason/contingency, life/art, language/truth, or nature/man. In the later period the tendency to paradox is further encouraged by his acceptance of contradictory Christian premises.

There also crop up certain specific difficulties, such as a certain mysteriousness, inevitably, when speaking of the Unknown, or the combination of certain Romantic ideas – especially in his American period – from Blake, Rimbaud, Rousseau and Kafka, combined with his Augustan tone, style and temperament. Another, acutely pointed out by Davison (*W. H. Auden*, 1970), lies in the very desire to simplify by using pop forms: they tend to involve the new poem in the cultural world of which they are a part. So if the author uses them perfectly he can't transcend them; if he doesn't, he seems to be satirising them by parody. In the later period, too, the use of rare words or logicless grammar, for special effects, may prove stumbling-blocks.

The beginning of sonnet XX of 'The Quest' illustrates the problem of symbolism:

> Within these gates all opening begins:
> White shouts and flickers through its green and red,
> Where children play at seven earnest sins
> And dogs believe their tall conditions dead.
>
> (*Collected Poems*, ed. Mendelson, p. 230)

Not an easy quatrain. 'Its' grammatically cannot refer to 'gates' and therefore must refer to 'opening', presumably the space within the gates. But what are the gates? Those of the senses? Or those of memory? Perhaps both (hence the deliberate vagueness?). 'White shouts and flickers' suggests a memory or vision of childhood innocence. The following quatrains seem to indicate that this is a potentiality which need not be restricted to childhood. But does 'green and red' point to innocence and experience, or spirit and body (blood), or just an Eden of leaf and flower? *Playing* at sins certainly confirms the idea of a symbolised state of innocence. But what about the last line?

'Tall conditions' are clearly the dogs' masters who restrict their freedom, but do they also stand for the Freudian superego, as Fuller says, and the dogs for the body? That might account for the odd implication that dogs would prefer their masters to be dead. 'Believe', of course, implies that they are *not* dead. Where does all that leave us? Probably with the impression that there never was a real state of innocence; the deadly sins were always lurking, we were never, and never would be, free of conditions and would not like it if we were, that there *is* some opposition of 'green' and 'red'; yet that such a state of free, harmonised integration is worth envisioning and striving towards. But it is difficult to be sure whether we are reading too much into this symbolic quatrain or too little.

The previous sonnet, however, splendidly conveys the essence and complexity of Auden's (and, the sonnet suggests, mankind's) major concern: to make sense of 'the baffle of being', of that 'Sole judge of truth, in endless error hurl'd /The glory, jest, and riddle of the world':

> Poet, oracle and wit
> Like unsuccessful anglers by
> The ponds of apperception sit,
> Baiting with the wrong request
> The vectors of their interest,
> At nightfall tell the angler's lie.
>
> With time in tempest everywhere,
> To rafts of frail assumption cling
> The saintly and the insincere;
> Enraged phenomena bear down
> In overwhelming waves to drown
> Both sufferer and suffering.
>
> The waters long to hear our question put
> Which would release their longed for answer, but.
>
> (Ibid.)

This is perfectly clear and rather clever; it metaphorises Auden's conceptual language sufficiently to prevent the poem from merely being a philosophical statement in verse but not so much as to obliterate the concepts; so that we get the *feeling* of baffling difficulty along with the statement of the problem. However, it does point towards two final sources of obscurity. The first is the use of rare words – of which *vectors* and *apperception* are mild examples – or of common words used in a rare sense, usually an older sense: witness '. . . Venus, to whose caprice/all blood must buxom' (bend, be obedient), or 'who wry from crowds' (turn, twist). The other, signalled by that final, open-ended 'but' is the use of what we may call logicless grammar – about which a little more needs to be said.

Sometimes a loss of logic is accepted simply for the sake of saving time; incorrect grammar is a shorthand-technique for packing more *meaning* (rather than more *sense-data*, in the imagist way) into a given verbal space:

> the sailors are not here because
> but only just-in-case
> ('Fleet Visit', *Collected Poems*, ed. Mendelson, p. 420)

> (Is there a once that is not already?)
> ('Not in Baedeker', Ibid. p. 422)

Sometimes they act as a modern equivalent of the eighteenth-century custom of reifying or slightly personifying abstractions: 'All that which lies outside our sort of why' has already been quoted in a different context. 'Pure scholarship in Where and When' ('The Sea and the Mirror') is one more example, of many to be found in the later period. More significantly, such playing with grammar seems particularly characteristic of poems dealing with imaginary lands, as in this stanza from the 'History of Science', which uses a fairy-tale structure to reinforce what this stanza implies, the element of luck in that history:

> Trusting some map in his own head,
> So never reached the goal intended
> (His map, of course, was out) but blundered
> On a wonderful instead.
> (*Collected Poems*, ed. Mendelson, p. 462)

A glance at the predicament Auden's Christian existentialism lands him in, makes it plain that he often needs more than the slight gain in solidity or brevity provided by such linguistic sleight of hand (which has to be paid for by cheques drawn on comprehensibility). What he needs is a way of unifying disparates, of putting over a difficult case, ultimately based on paradox and pure faith. He must contemplate the objectivity of the objective world and the subjectivity of the chosen self within it, and present the result as a compound apprehension. A task complicated by uncertainty as to the right nature of the self, the right status of a fallen, but innocent Nature, and a belief that no worldly particular is *ultimately* better or worse than any other (though *proximately* it may be). The combination of an imaginary, metaphysical land with a stage-magician's grammar can greatly assist that task. The companion piece to the 'History of Science', given the significantly provocative title 'The History of Truth', perfectly illustrates that point. It is also probably Auden's most difficult poem; but given some knowledge of his later beliefs and grammatical habits it can be teased out in detail. For present purposes, however, a partial interpretation will be enough:

> In that ago, when being was believing,
> Truth was the most of many credibles,

More first, more always, than a bat-winged lion,
A fish-tailed dog, or eagle-headed fish,
The least like mortals, doubted by their deaths.

Truth was their model as they strove to build
A world of lasting objects to believe in,
Without believing earthenware and legend,
Archway and song were truthful or untruthful:
The Truth was there already to be true.

This while when, practical like paper-dishes,
Truth is convertible to kilowatts,
Our last to do by is an anti-model,
Some untruth anyone can give the lie to,
A nothing no one need believe is there.
                    (*Collected Poems*, ed. Mendelson, p. 463)

This is a version of the Two Truths theory. There is a practical or empirical truth, revisable in the light of experiment or new experience, and there is a spiritual truth, outside the confines of empiricism, and therefore neither falsifiable nor verifiable by empirical methods. Since the first truth is more obviously 'true' by normal standards, exceptional weapons are needed to defend the less obvious truth, and indeed to maintain its superiority, as Auden wishes. The technique is to move us subtly into a non-land, where the fact that we are really dealing with two entirely different meanings of the word 'truth' will be disguised, and where the first meaning can be shown at a disadvantage (for that meaning is designed to deal with the material world). Each stanza, therefore, starts with the physical and turns itself inside-out to end in the metaphysical, an easy process since, despite the emphasis on 'being', time and place as we know them have disappeared. 'They' who 'strove to build a world of lasting objects to believe in' cannot be placed as any particular people, nor their world as any particular place.

In the first phrase, 'ago', an adverb, is not used as a noun for brevity's sake. 'In that age' would have done. Its effect is to generate a slight feeling of queerness: this is not a time in history, but an imaginary space-time with hints of Classical Greece, Ancient Egypt, and Medieval Europe. A queerness developed by the existentialist pun on seeing and being, which leads to the paradox of equating being and believing – though of course the fairly similar idea of a lived truth as opposed to an understood truth is not novel. 'Credibles' by being made plural is also turned from an adjective into a noun, and thus comes to suggest things, existents, though all it can really mean is 'logically, if not empirically, credible stories'. This usage tends to lead us to do the same with 'the most' ('Truth was the tops'). By the time we come to the last line of the stanza, however, we realise that it must also mean 'the most credible' (contrasted with 'the least' credible). So the least credible religions died like mortals and thus cast doubt on their validity, and the religions 'least like mortals' (bat-winged etc.) died out. 'The Truth was there already to be true' is a crucial example. The capital 'T' helps us to take the non-empirical truth as some sort of thing, an existent. 'The truth was there all ready to be true' implies that potentiality becomes fact, the truth, when embodied in objects; and 'The Truth was there already' implies that it existed as a model in some other realm, which could be imitated without the believers mistaking the imitation for the original. The contrast with the present day ('This while when' rather than 'These days when') is then easy to effect in terms that paradoxically turn the materialistic 'truth' into a mere nothing.

Problems in Auden, then, are rarely quite insoluble. Whether the most problematic poems are worth the effort of solution is a moot point. In general – and admitting many exceptions – it seems true to say that the least dogmatic and theoretical work of both periods tends to be the best. Where he ponders his subjects and themes with his eye more on the facts than on political or religious theory, he most often realises his potential as the last truly major poet writing in English – perhaps the last we shall ever have, for all later poets have grown up in a culture increasingly visual rather than verbal.

Themes and Treatment

Some poets tend to deal in subjects but not themes; that is to say that the material of the poem is unrelated to any idea or preoccupation. Auden is not that sort of poet. His very varied subjects are normally related to one or more of a number of preoccupations; such as (in the Thirties) love, politics, peace, neurosis, death, fear, and character, or (after the Thirties) love, technology and social engineering, nature, the Good Life, man in essence, history, and the nature of art. These are not dealt with for their own sake, to evoke or freshen what they feel like, but rather for their significance. Not necessarily a simple significance, yielding an unqualified message. On the contrary, as we have suggested, they are commonly seen in terms of tension, dualism, or complexity – indeed, that they have to be seen in such terms often *is* the theme.

Whether subject-matter, as it were, simply rests where it falls or comes to suggest a theme is largely a matter of treatment: in particular a message, a moral, or an abstract idea may be somewhere stated, or a motif (such as that of danger in the 'Consider' passage: *hawk*, *airman*, *smouldering*, *insufficient*, *dangerous*) may impel us to look beyond naturalism; or else symbolic material (myth, psychological landscape) may remove the subject from the realm of realism.

For this reason, then, themes and treatment cannot sensibly be taken in isolation. For much the same reason it will not be profitable to treat Auden's highly distinctive use of myth, nature, and imagery in total separation from each other or from the matter of theme. The same kind of images may be used to embody different themes, the same theme be embodied in different kinds of imagery. Nature may be mythicised, history and myth may be intermingled. On the other hand, certain kinds of versification may have no particular relevance to the subject or the theme of a poem; they simply exist as a pleasure in their own right. Hence, such topics will be separately dealt with only in so far as that is convenient.

Certain themes – in the sense of *preoccupations* – recur in both the earlier and later periods. In each case, however, the theme, in the sense of *message*, differs in the two periods. Most notable are preoccupations with the Quest, the Duality of Man, the Goodness of Sex, the difference between Animals (or Nature) and Man, the Integration of Personality, the Need to trust something other than Reason, and the relation of Art and Reality. Naturally some of these merge with each other. For example, the quest may well be a quest for personal integration.

In the English period the quest is for a new *society*, though admittedly this is not seen as independent of a new self. Auden never fully accepted the Marxist view that men are what they are wholly by reason of their environment. Indeed his references to a death wish in the bourgeoisie and the need for personal rebirth in those who would lead the way to the promised land often suggest the opposite. However, the chief end in view remains that of a new society, which will arise from the ruins of the old. Later on, it becomes a quest for a new *life*, signified in its full form by a Kierkegaardian journey from the aesthetic through the ethical, to the religious state; the Just City now being no more than an unattainable though approachable ideal.

Similarly man's duality is at first located mainly in the disparity between his Superego and Id, the moral consciousness and the chthonic powers; later, it is located rather more traditionally in the disparities of body and spirit, or the difference between what men wish to be like and what they actually are. Sex is at first to be taken as a good in that it tends towards psychological, and indeed physical health; and, moreover, may lead to the general social love that the new society will require. Later, sexual love is acceptable because it may lead to the love of God. Again, animals at first are envied because, unlike man, they live in a natural environment to which they are wholly attuned, and lacking foreknowledge, have no fear of death or sense of impending doom. Later, they are envied and a little despised *because* they have no foreknowledge – or guilt or morality. They are innocent but cannot be virtuous. So with the integration of personality: it will come from self-knowledge and will be of value both in its own right and in so far as it may contribute to creating the new secular society. A view that gradually transforms itself into the idea of the need for authenticity in order to be fully human and the need to be fully human in order to be properly Christian.

Time, in the English period, is usually seen as the enemy because it is rapidly running out, or, looking backwards, because it is responsible for the deadening and deadly system of Christianity and capitalism which created the tradition that prevents reform. In the American period, it is more usually regarded as a necessary complement to eternity. Trusting something, other than reason, starts by being Freudian – the need not to repress unwelcome knowledge or feeling into the unconscious where it can wreak havoc unperceived – and becomes Kierkegaardian – the need to trust in the Absurd (eventually to take the leap in the dark, to Faith). Finally, to put it crudely, art is at first either a psychological compensation or a means of influencing opinion. Later, it is at best an imitation of God the supreme artist, alone able to reconcile fully the contraries of life. At second-best, a verbal game that may by its exemplary structuring and by luck and grace (also the way integration of the personality in this period is to come about) point the way to such reconciliation.

There are, of course, complications. All these themes tend to crop up in partial or disguised forms, and all could be stated in different terms. Furthermore, Auden was never a wholly committed didactic writer. As Justin Replogle says in *Auden's Poetry*, when the Poet becomes too highfaluting an unromantic Antipoet emerges to take him down a peg. In his later period, too, Auden was well aware of the pernicious possibilities of Christianity:

> Reluctant at first
> to break his sworn promise
> of Safe Conduct, after
>
> consulting his confessor,
> in good spirits
> he signed a death-warrant

('Marginalia', *Collected Poems*, p. 594)

> *Be godly*, he told his flock,
> *bloody and extreme*
> *like the Holy Ghost.*

(Ibid. p. 595)

And, contrariwise, if his later attitude to the planned collective society was scathing, it was no more than an extension of the scepticism lurking in the Thirties. 'Preserve me from the Shape of Things to Be . . .' has already been quoted from the 'Letter to Lord Byron' (p. 28). Add to all this, Auden's belief that poets should not be simple, on purely literary grounds, and the need to use generalisations with caution is evident:

> Be subtle, various, ornamental, clever,
> And do not listen to those critics ever
> Whose crude, provincial gullets crave in books
> Plain cooking made still plainer by plain cooks.
>
> ('The Truest Poetry is the most Feigning', Ibid. p. 470)

In general, it seems true to say that Auden's poetry becomes more complex both in themes and treatment as he goes on – a fact that makes the greater clarity of the later work an achievement all the more remarkable. More and more, that is to say, the themes become interconnected, so that poems express more than one strand of his web of preoccupations; and techniques become more elaborate and clever (though skilfully less obtrusive) as the poet comes to think of himself more as craftsman and entertainer than as healer of a sick society, and to think of poetry as game rather than sermon, ornamental rather than functional.

Necessary qualifications to this oversimplification have already been made. It remains to add only that the stylistic difference is in any case merely relative. Auden's technical ability, for instance, was always exceptional – as a brief look at one conveniently extractable aspect of it will indicate.

Auden's Imagery

His images almost always tend to make one *see* more than feel or sense, but within that limitation there is a range in the English period alone of at least a dozen different kinds. Some simply strike the reader as fresh and brilliant; a great imaginative leap bridges apparently utterly unlike entities in a way that clears the scales of habit from the mind's eye:

> But thinking so I came at once
> Where solitary man sat weeping on a bench,
> Hanging his head down, with mouth distorted
> Helpless and ugly as an embryo chicken
>
> (*The English Auden*, ed. Mendelson, p. 37)

The lack of an indefinite article before 'solitary' hints that mankind is essentially solitary, each man an island – a state Auden later came to think less easily correctible. 'Ugly' is apt for the embryo, and it permits pity without any sentimentalising of grief. The whole physical attitude graphically portrays the intensity of despair, while the 'embryo' allows the possibility of growth, improvement, birth into a new life.

> ... fallen bicycles like huddled corpses
>
> (Op.cit. p. 37)

Again, a likeness one would never have thought of that nevertheless suddenly brings into focus the casual-seeming inhuman horror of those newsreel heaps. Psychological imagery, like 'the liar's quinsy' is common, as are dream images used as social symbols:

Have things gone too far already? Are we done for? Must we
    wait
Hearing doom's approaching footsteps regular down miles of
    straight

(Op.cit. p. 49)

The touch of fantastic humour in this nightmare image is not uncharacteristic of the social poetry. Panoramic imagery is everywhere:

> Here on the cropped grass of the narrow ridge I stand,
> A fathom of earth, alive in air,
> Aloof as an admiral on the old rocks,
> England below me ...

(Op.cit. p. 141)

Why not a general? Not only because an admiral does stand high up on the bridge of his flagship, but also precisely because our attention should not be deflected from the *idea* (of aloofness) to the *scene*. The description of the narrator as 'a fathom of earth' further removes us from emotional human involvement; we are to take a god's-eye view. Sometimes indeed a view so long that man is dwarfed rather than quasi-divinely elevated like the admiral:

> ... the planets
> Continue their circulations; and the galaxy
> Is free for ever to revolve like an enormous biscuit

(Op.cit. p. 262)

Or *is* man dwarfed? Do we find, in the last phrase, the Antipoet cutting the universe down to size?

Beyond this one cannot go – save by passing out of imagery altogether; and indeed this sense of the panoramic does seem to be related to another of Auden's great gifts, that of memorable generalisation. Note, for instance, from the English period such lines as these:

> ... the hospitals alone remind us
> Of the equality of man.

(Op.cit. p. 261)

> Or hum of printing presses turning forests into lies

(Op.cit. p. 269)

A largely political observation, bearing within it something of the later ecological interest in man and nature. From the American period:

> Earth's mishaps are not fatal,
> Fire is not quenched by the dark,
> no one can bottle a Breeze,
> no friction wear out Water
> (*Collected Poems*, ed. Mendelson, p. 665)

Here the interest lies entirely in the idea, not the diction. Whether or not we relate this to Auden's later theology, it does neatly use the traditional four elements to indicate that the 'Absurd' (the fact that things are purely contingent and have no logical reason for being as they are) can be a cause for rejoicing. Or, again:

> The yoke permitted
> Gentle dray horses to build
> Coercive castles
> (Ibid. p. 552)

A large implication is seen in one small invention, and the other side of contingent 'absurdity' is snapshot for us.

A quite different kind of imagery is that which is akin to stage-setting or lighting. This kind is central to 'The Capital', which will be examined later. Then there is what may be called archetypal imagery. Witness the 'He' of the sonnet sequence of *In Time of War* (*English Auden* pp. 251–262) which stands for Mankind, or representative types of Man (peasant, poet, hero, witch-doctor/scientist, civiliser), or the Superego/God. Both compound or punning images and allegorically symbolic imagery are common. Both are represented in this stanza from 'As I walked out one evening':

> Into many a green valley
>   Drifts the appalling snow;
> Time breaks the threaded dances
> And the diver's brilliant bow.
> (Ibid. p. 228)

The snow is at once horrifying and acting as a pall of death. The green valley, the dances, and the diving seem to represent nature, art, and physical ability; all subject to the attack of time. Animal and nature imagery is so frequent as to need no illustration, and in any case must inevitably figure in any discussion of themes and treatment – as must imagery drawn from legend, fairy-tale, or Auden's own home-made myth (discussed in Part One), which must also feature largely in discussion of themes and treatment. So largely in fact that a preliminary paragraph or two on what we may call Auden's mythicising will not come amiss as an introduction to that discussion.

All these kinds of imagery continue into the American period, where they join company with others. All of them too tend, as one would expect, to take on different colouring or implication as the themes of the poetry change in emphasis and in the degree of their interconnectedness. Of none is this more true than of the mythic kind of imagery – though fortunately Auden has a relatively clear and straightforward idea of myth.

Auden's Myths

Before 1900, two views of the nature of myth were in competition: the realist and the idealist. Realists took a pragmatic view of myth: it was a primitive attempt at history, or at doctrinal or moral allegory, or it was a distorted deification of natural forces. Idealists saw myth as the embodiment of transcendental realities or of subconscious intuitions or drives that would otherwise be inaccessible. After 1900, the two views tend to mingle. Myth is taken to represent a sort of dream-thought (an early evolutionary form on the way to rational thinking). It may be thought about the inner or the outer world, or both, for the two do interact, but, in either cases, thought to be experienced rather than interpreted. It is taken to embody what is timeless and universal in human experience as against what is temporal and local. One can well see why Auden, with his inclination to the overview, should incline to this mingling – although really up-to-date anthropologists seem to distrust all generalisations about myths, preferring to view them separately in their local contexts.

In *Forewords and Afterwords* ('Grimm and Andersen') Auden says three different things about fairy-stories. Firstly, that they are a form of moral thought: the right sort of characters (especially uncalculating goodhearted third sons) attract luck, justice triumphs, good .is rewarded, evil punished. Secondly, that they are a dramatic projection of what lurks in the primitive depths of the mind (i.e. are a form of amoral, or even immoral thought – certainly many of Grimm's tales are grim indeed); representing what is rather than what ought to be, or, what we ought not to wish – but somewhere perhaps do. Thirdly, he says that Hans Andersen's tales are more literary – parables rather than myths proper, in that they explain their symbols. Hans Andersen's, we may interpret, correspond more to the first, moral, class and express the conscious mind; Grimm's, the second, psychological kind, and express the subconscious. Two subdivisions, then, of 'expressive' myth.

In *The Dyer's Hand*, he writes:

> To believe in Aphrodite and Ares merely means that one believes that the poetic myths about them do justice to the forces of sex and aggression as human beings experience them in nature and their own lives . (pp. 456–7)

Here myth is clearly taken to be also 'explanatory' – and it is evident from the poetry that 'nature' is taken to include an urban

86

environment, in fact to cover anything that is not inside man himself. In each case, myth in Auden turns out to be a special form of imagery, rationally chosen, to enable writer and reader to respond sensuously and emotionally to the facts of life, inner or outer. It is symbolic metaphor writ large, since it makes the abstract concrete, and the concrete general. There is nowhere any indication of primitive *belief* in myth; indeed, late in his career Auden doubts whether there ever was:

> ... I'd swear
> that men have always lounged in myths
> as Tall Stories.

('Archaeology', *Collected Poems*, ed. Mendelson, p. 662)

The use of myth, then, allows the abstract and general to be dramatised and particularised, and if necessary touched with comic exaggeration to make its point the more graphically.

When Auden uses Clio, the goddess of history, to symbolise Time, or contrasts Artemis and Aphrodite (representing the body) with Hermes and Apollo (the mind), or refers to dragons, ogres, or giantesses, it is obvious that we are in the realm of the mythic. But what about mixed history? Those poems which seem to use concrete instances to suggest a hypothetical or typical society: tottering empire, as in 'The Fall of Rome', or more subtly, typical dictatorship, as in 'Epitaph on a Tyrant'?:

> Perfection, of a kind, was what he was after,
> And the poetry he invented was easy to understand;
> He knew human folly like the back of his hand,
> And was greatly interested in armies and fleets;
> When he laughed, respectable senators burst with laughter,
> And when he cried the little children died in the streets.

(Op.cit. p. 149)

In 1939, he and his readers would undoubtedly have Hitler and Mussolini in mind, and possibly Stalin, but 'Epitaph' indicates a dead tyrant; 'senators' would fit modern Italy but probably is more suggestive of ancient Rome – especially as 'the poetry' reminds us of Nero. And the internal rhyme in the last line, on reflection, seems to encapsulate the horrific essence of any dictatorship: that the people are subject not to justice but whim; the melancholy ruler can take it out on the innocent. This sort of thing certainly seems to be an extension of what we may call the myth-method. A further, equally logical, extension would include all Auden's archetypal poems – and in this way something akin to the myth-method seeps into the majority of his poems in that they tend to use concrete, but *not* specific examples to embody general concepts. The examples, that is to say, are in Time and Place but not *a* time and place.

To return to themes and treatment: myths, legends and fairy-tales not uncommonly involve a quest. So any Quest poem, even if it does not refer specifically to legendary beings, or 'essential history', takes on some tinge of myth.

Quests

'O where are you going?' (op.cit. p. 60) is a very early example of the quest-theme economically used, inseparably interwoven with the theme of integration (both personal and social) and treated already with consummate technical skill. The opening question gives us the quest-theme, as does the word 'rider' in the first line; the ballad-form reminds us of many narratives of dangers undergone for some great purpose. The alliterative method, here fused with rhyme, takes us back to particularly dire and dangerous times – perhaps to the alliterative *Gawain and the Green Knight*, a quest-narrative whose symbolic essence is largely internal: the quest being really a search for perfection of character. Certain of the details are surely deliberately evocative of Browning's *Childe Roland*, which implies as does Auden's ballad the need for dauntlessness in the face of overwhelming odds. 'Reader' in the first line sets up the contrast between the apathetic and the active in society – though the last stanza, together with the mythic nightmarish aura of the poem as a whole, leaves one fairly sure that all the contrasting qualities are to be found in the self as well as in society:

> 'O where are you going?' said reader to rider,
> 'That valley is fatal when furnaces burn,
> Yonder's the midden whose odours will madden,
> That gap is the grave where the tall return.'...
>
> 'O do you imagine,' said fearer to farer,
> That dusk will delay on your path to the pass ...

It comes as no surprise to find that decades later Auden became a Tolkien fan.

'The Exiles' (*English Auden*, p. 98), however, is a much more puzzling poem, perhaps because Auden has not chosen to take much advantage of the dramatic simplification of myth. Instead of fearer and farer dramatising in dialogue both internal and social differences, they are here mingled in such a way that it is difficult to say whether the poem is complex or confused. Perhaps the truth is that it confuses complexity where the ballad clarified it. The poem starts as if it were to be about a genuine quest, a self-imposed exile from bourgeois security and complacency:

> What siren zooming is sounding our coming
> Up frozen fjord forging from freedom ...

O who can ever praise enough
   The world of his belief?
Harum-scarum childhood plays
In the meadows near his home,
In his woods love knows no wrong,
Travellers ride their placid ways,
In the cool shade of the tomb
Age's trusting footfalls ring.
O who can paint the vivid tree
   And grass of phantasy?

But to create it and to guard
   Shall be his whole reward.
He shall watch and he shall weep,
All his father's love deny,
To his mother's womb be lost,
Eight nights with a wanton sleep,
But upon the ninth shall be
Bride and victim to a ghost,
And in the pit of terror thrown
   Shall bear the wrath alone.

W. H. Auden

Auden's manuscript of a poem containing hints of questing, fairy-tale and mythicising

The second stanza seems to confirm this, as we:

> Advance to meet
> Each new recruit.

Again, the alliterative patterning of the longer lines in each stanza gives the thing an air of craggy Anglo-Saxon toughness. But why 'forging *from* freedom'? One might think that to be just what those working for a Marxist society are doing, but it was not what left-wing radicals would have said in the Thirties, however much they might have deplored certain aspects of capitalist freedom. Soon, too, the suggestion of a guerilla army in exile takes on overtones of a holiday-camp, which then pass into anticipations of picnics in July and charades at Christmas, and we end, explicitly, back in London – at any rate in the original version; the *Collected Poems* version omits a number of stanzas and revises the last one in such a way as to suggest that the poem records a purely internal quest – which is rather inconsistent with 'recruits', 'In groups forgetting the gun in the drawer', and the constant use of the plural 'Our'. Both versions seem to record an Alice-through-the-looking-glass quest where the illusion of pressing on disguises the fact of going backwards. The hints of the Thirties' new myth in the phrases mentioned certainly suggest a common effort at social change. The rest of the poem suggests total failure, without however indicating any reason for it. One or two stanzas might refer to the process of getting older:

> We shall never need another new outfit;
> These grounds are for good, we shall grow no more,
>> But lose our colour
>> With scurf on collar
>> Peering through glasses
>> At our own glosses.

or
>> Saying Alas
>> To less and less

But one must obviously take this as symbolical of a lapse back from 'farer' to 'fearer' – a psychological failure of will related, by (admittedly rather unclear) implication, to political action. The revision of the last stanza so as to include the statement 'their now is a time/Too late for love or for lying either' seems to attempt to eliminate the social element, but succeeds only in muddying a never quite clarified poem.

'As He Is' (1937) is a more coherent poem, perhaps because the subject of the quest is to be seen satirically as the second stanza makes clear, so his quest must be a false one:

> Beneath the hot unasking sun,
>> Past stronger beasts and fairer
> He picks his way, a living gun,
>> With gun and lens and Bible,
>> A militant enquirer,
> The friend, the rash, the enemy,
>> The essayist, the able,
>> Able at times to cry
> (*Collected Poems*, ed. Mendelson, p. 142)

90

This quest is related only to matters of personal integration and authenticity, so it naturally enough assimilates something of Auden's thinking on animals and nature which forms the main theme of many poems. This stanza compares him unfavourably with other beasts, but, anticipating the later attitude to animals, does allow him the capacity to write and to cry, which implies a greater *potentiality* than they have. Future false-quest themes are anticipated in the conclusion to this poem, a conclusion quite compatible with the notion of potentiality, namely, that by defeat in a false quest he may come to the truth, by 'further griefs and greater' come to the 'defeat of grief'. Sonnet XIII, in the long sonnet sequence 'The Quest', offers a variation on this theme by asserting the usefulness of failed heroes to others. It starts with mythic images of the various disasters the quester is prone to: 'The over-logical fell for the witch/Whose argument converted him to stone'; and it ends with the consolation that 'even madmen manage to convey/Unwelcome truths in lonely gibberish'.

Some indication of the way themes gradually become parts of an increasingly integrated web of thought or preoccupations can be gathered if we start with the latter part of a poem from 1940:

> All his lifetime he will find
> Swollen knee or aching tooth
> Hostile to his quest for truth;
> Never will his prick belong
> To his world of right and wrong,
> Nor its values comprehend
> Who is foe and who is friend.

('Shorts', *Collected Poems*, ed. Mendelson, p. 232)

The association of 'truth' with 'right and wrong' implies that the poem is concerned with a quest for integration, a better self. This question, however, is integrally connected with the 'absurd' or, more neutrally speaking, contingent nature of the world, and that in turn is inseparable from the body/spirit conflict, which is itself inseparable from the tension between what men are and what they ought to be or wish to be. Several areas of thought are woven together into one complex theme.

Quant's remark, in *The Age of Anxiety* (1947), seems limited to the theme of the absurd.

> No soul is safe. Let slight infection
> Disturb a trifle some tiny gland,
> And Caustic Keith grows kind and silly
> Or Dainty Daisy dirties herself.
> We are mocked by unmeaning; among us fall
> Aimless arrows, hurting at random
> As we plan to pain.   (Ibid. p. 363)

But 'No soul' clearly means more than 'Nobody', and 'As we plan to pain' admits the possibility of ordered evil (for the quest may be a perverse one). However, the quest theme attaches to this brief passage, in a much more complicated way, by context. For the four characters of the work represent the Jungian divisions of the personality: Intuition (Quant), Thought (Malin), Feeling (Rosetta), and Sensation (Emble), and the entire long poem consists of a quest for integration – a quest that involves several false quests, and touches on the fact that Art, which is ordered, may be set against contingency, absurdity, just as 'truth' can, and indeed may be a better model for integration. This last thematic variation, however, is much more fully developed in the equally long 'Sea and the Mirror'. But before looking briefly at that work we might profitably spend a little time in looking at the way the Quest-theme of the *Age of Anxiety* fuses with the themes of Nature and Time. The four characters come to a dead end (a graveyard) and find a message, the latter part of which reads as follows:

> Here impulse loses
> Its impetus: thus
> Far and no farther
> Their legs, resolutions
> And longings carried
> The big, the ambitious,
> The beautiful; all
> Stopped in mid-stride
> At this straggling border
> Where wildflowers begin
> And wealth ends.
>
> Yet around their rest
> Flittermice, finches
> And flies restore
> Their lost milieu;
> An inconsequential
> Host of pert
> Occasional creatures,
> Blindly, playfully,
> Bridging death's
> Eternal gap
> With quotidian joy.
> (Op.cit. p. 384)

Are they wrong to stop here where wealth ends? Surely not, one feels; a return to nature must bring about some resolution of the disharmony produced by the pursuit of wealth in an industrial society. After all, the country creatures are in tune with their milieu and live in daily joy. This would be in keeping with the sentiments of, say, the Chorus in *The Dog Beneath the Skin* ('Happy the hare at morning . . .') or 'Fish in the unruffled lakes', in which creatures other than man are envied for their innocence and freedom from dread. But 'their lost milieu' is ambiguous; it could refer to the questers. True, it might well imply the restoration of a primitive milieu that industrial man has lost – and this would be retrogressive. The creatures are 'inconsequential', 'pert', 'occasional', 'Blind', all rather disparaging words; and 'quotidian' means not only daily but also commonplace. In this way, questions of body and spirit, Is and Ought are made to hover in the mind. And on the very next page crossing this sort of border is seen as a *temptation*:

> These old-world hamlets and haphazard lanes
> Are perilous places; how plausible here
> All arcadian cults of carnal perfection,
> How intoxicating the platonic myth.

Perhaps instead a very different, inner landscape should be attempted that will lead out of the quotidian into a sense of eternity:

> Rosetta says:
>   Are our dreams indicative? Does it exist
>   That last landscape
>   Of gloom and glaciers and great storms
>   Where, cold into chasms, cataracts
>   Topple . . .
>
>   Can lying lovers believe their bones'
>   Unshaken assurance
>   That all the elegance, all the promise
>   Of the world they wish is waiting there?
>   (Op.cit. p. 391)

The nice pun on 'lying' allows the possibility of coming to the spiritual through the physical, or transmuting apparent opposites. This Icelandic, nightmarish vision is far from Rosetta's earlier, backward-looking day-dream of her (imaginary) arcadian past:

> We beheld what was ours. Undulant land
> Rose layer by layer till at last the sea
> Far away flashed; from fretted uplands
> That lay to the north, from limestone heights
> Incisive rains had dissected well,
> For down each dale industrious there ran
> A paternoster of ponds and mills,
> Came sweet waters, assembling quietly

By a clear congress of accordant streams
A mild river that moseyed at will
Through parks and ploughland, purring southward
In a wide valley . . .
                    sheep grazed in
The ancient hollows of meander scars and
Long-legged ladies with little-legged dogs
Lolled with their lovers by lapsing brooks.
A couth region . . .
Where country curates in cold bedrooms
Dreamed of deaneries till at daybreak
The rector's rooks with relish described
Their stinted station.

(Op.cit. pp. 347–8)

The quest is not a theme of this passage, save in so far as it lies behind all passages of *The Age of Anxiety*. Apart from that context, perhaps, we are more likely to see latent in it the theme of art and reality. For clearly this lovely English landscape is a pastoral painting in words. Though it shares with the 'Icelandic' passages and 'O where are you going' the alliterative method of early English poetry, it has neither the consonantal clatter of the one nor the curt cross-talk of the other. Rosetta's memory is fondly, and far from ignobly, creative. There is no satire or condemnation here – but there is a gentle comedy that at once celebrates nature (civilised nature) and sees it as a temptation to escapism. Not that this is an *impossible* countryside; here and there in eighteenth-century England certain places approached such a pastoral couthness; and certainly it is an improvement on Rosetta's life in New York. But the touch of comedy about the curate, the deliberately precious words like 'couth' and 'moseyed', the brilliant but ever so slightly incongruous imaginative leap from ponds and mills to 'paternoster', from streams to an accordant congress, hint at the pursuit of delight rather than truth – which is where the question of art and reality most obviously comes in.

'The Sea and the Mirror'

'The Sea and the Mirror' goes deeply into this question; so deeply that a complete book could well be written on its probings. A brief examination of a few passages, however, should suffice to conclude this disquisition on the interweaving of themes, and may cast a useful light on Auden's poetic method in general.

In 'Caliban to the Audience', the long, elaborately wrought section of Jamesian prose, which shows Caliban to be really more sophisticated than Ariel or even Prospero, we start by asking why Shakespeare should have introduced brute reality (Caliban) into a work of the spirit (Ariel), distorting its ordered beauty. This is countered by the contention that if poetry intruded into life it would prove far more disruptive than the intrusion of life into poetry. Ariel is also a form of Cupid, Christ, and, by reason of his creativity and the capital letter always given to his personal pronoun, God: that is to say, he is the god-in-oneself (which *can* order the inner world in a way that the outer world of contingency cannot be ordered – though we do need to react to it by constant efforts of structuring akin to those of art). It is easy to see that the god-in-oneself could easily produce daydream, wishful fantasies, and works of art comparable to them – things different in kind, though dangerously similar in appearance, to structurings that incorporate reality in a higher synthesis. Not surprisingly, then, we find that *Caliban* also is assimilated to Cupid and God, and to Ariel; all of them, after all, being inseparable elements of the self. In this way, the themes of order/contingency, What Is/the Wholly Other, and spirit/body are involved in the subject of art/reality. At this point the quest-theme comes in, symphonically. The aspiring artist – and who, if he aspires to be human, is not one? – is shown on two quests, both failures: into the immediate (the 'Caliban' quest) and into the possible (the 'Ariel'). They cannot be fully harmonised in this life, and the aspirant is ironically advised against any strenuous attempt to do so. He should stop at the station, where he will have all the pleasure of feeling himself a quester without the dire problems:

> you will never meet a jollier, more various crowd than you see around you here, sharing with you the throbbing, suppressed excitement of those to whom the exciting thing is still, perhaps, to happen. But once you leave, no matter in which direction, your next stop will be far outside this land of habit that so democratically stands up for your right to stagestruck hope.
>
> (*Collected Poems*, ed. Mendelson, p. 335)

If he persists, he will find himself in a state of existential dread, where he must choose, but where Ariel and Caliban can no longer guide and advise, but only obey. He will be out on his own:

> 'Release us,' you will beg . . . 'release us from our minor roles. Carry me back, Master, to the cathedral town where the canons run through the water meadows with butterfly nets and the old women keep sweetshops in the cobbled side streets, or back to the upland mill town (gunpowder and plush) with its grope-movie and its poolroom lit by gas, carry me back to the days before my wife put on weight, back to the years when beer was cheap and the rivers really froze in winter. Pity me Captain, pity a poor old stranded sea-salt . . .

And in that very moment when you so cry for deliverance from any and every anxious possibility, I shall have no option ... but to transport you, not indeed to any cathedral town or mill town or harbour or hillside or jungle or other specific Eden which your memory necessarily but falsely conceives of as the ultimate liberal condition, which in point of fact you have never known yet, but directly to that downright state itself ... Directly overhead a full moon casts a circle of dazzling light without any penumbra, exactly circumscribing its desolation in which every object is extraordinarily still and sharp. Cones of extinct volcanoes rise up abruptly from the lava plateau fissured by chasms ... Here ... at long last you are, as you have asked to be, the only subject.

(Ibid. pp. 336–7)

Two passages almost exactly equivalent to those of Rosetta; the first mildly mocking a self-deceptive nostalgia, the second briefly ironic about the irresponsible, uncivilised unconditioned 'free' self. The quest-theme, again inextricably entangled with preoccupations about art, reality, authenticity and nature.

This hell-like Icelandic landscape is no more to be despised than to be comfortably avoided, however. It presents an untampered-with truth, and the chance of a fresh start. It may be uncomfortable, but it is also unspoilt. Hence it is to be valued; but so is 'art', an agent of 'cultivation'. Writing on the bleakness of Hammerfest Auden concludes, in 1961:

> Ground so bare might take a century to realise
>   How we behave to regions or to beings
> Who have anything we're after: to have disgusted
>   Millions of acres of good-natured topsoil
> Is an achievement of a sort, to fail to notice
>   How garden plants and farmyard beasts look at us,
> Or refuse to look, to picture all of them as dear
>   Faithful old retainers, another, but why
> Bring that up now? My intrusion had not profaned it:
>   If innocence is holy, it was holy.

(Op.cit. p. 545)

And in *New Year Letter* (op.cit. p. 162) he places the role of art with extraordinary clarity and insight:

> For art had set in order sense
> And feeling and intelligence,
> And from its ideal order grew
> *Our local understanding too* [*italics added*]
> ....
> Art in intention is mimesis
> But, realised, the resemblance ceases;
> Art is not life and cannot be

96

A midwife to society, [*A change from the Thirties' view*]
For art is a *fait accompli.*.
What they should do, or how or when
Life-order comes to living men
It cannot say, for it presents
Already lived experience
Through a convention that creates
Autonomous completed states,
Though their particulars are those
That each particular artist knows,
Unique events that once took place
Within a unique time and space,
In the new field they occupy,
The unique serves to typify,
Becomes, though still particular,
An algebraic formula,
An abstract model of events
Derived from dead experience,
And each life must itself decide
To what and how it be applied [*italics added*]

Of nature (and man) without art he writes:

Whether they thought of Nature, of her unending stream of
irrelevant events without composition or centre, her reckless waste
of value, her alternate looks of idiot inertia and insane ferocity, or
whether they thought of Man, of the torpor of his spirit, the indigent
dryness of his soul, his bottomless credulity, his perverse preference
for the meretricious or the insipid . . .

(*The Age of Anxiety*, Op.cit. p. 393)

So 'nature', like myth (sometimes in fact itself mythicised) occurs as
a form of imagery to embody or point up thematic preoccupations
with man's difference and similarity, with society, with integration, as
well as with art. Thus, in complex rhyming stanzas, Alonso warns
Ferdinand against royal egotism:

But keep in mind the waters where fish
See sceptres descending with no wish
To touch them . . .

Remember as bells and cannon boom
The cold deep that does not envy you,
The sunburnt superficial kingdom
Where a king is an object
(*The Sea and the Mirror*, Op.cit. p. 320)

In 'Musée des Beaux Arts' whose main theme is the incorporation in
great art of profound perceptions about life, animals ('nature') come in

only incidentally, but carry a weight of judgement against man. The 'dreadful martyrdom' runs its course:

> Where the dogs go on with their doggy life and the torturer's horse
> Scratches its innocent behind on a tree.
>
> (Op.cit. p. 146)

The easy-going, understressed lines, like nature itself, play down and absorb the horror – thereby making it subtly more horrible; again, nature's passive innocence is not good enough. Only some active virtue could prove remedial; but the line-length suggests life's trivial pottering on.

'Their Lonely Betters' combines themes of animals, man's dualism, and art. Language is seen as the really differentiating factor; it makes man capable of lying, and rhyming, of keeping or breaking promises. He is thus better, but lonelier, alienated from the world by having 'assumed responsibility for time' instead of living like other creatures in an eternal physical present. Overtly the poem celebrates man's superiority, but the muted rhythm, the element of paradox (lying as a sign of superiority), and certain juxtapositions, cast a shadow over the celebration. This kind of wry comedy is to be found in a rather wittier form in 'Reflections in a Forest' (op.cit. p. 504), in which complexity of idea and lucidity of expression go hand in hand:

> Within a shadowland of trees
> Whose lives are so uprightly led
> In nude august communities,
> To move about seems underbred.

Without the slightest hint of didacticism man, nature, and morality are introduced, and the mode of witty comedy is set. 'Shadowland' not only calls up the cool quality of woods but suggests that their world is a negative image of ours. 'Uprightly' puns on the physical and moral; men too go upright, unlike animals, but unupright behaviour is hardly so unthinkable for them as it is for trees. The comic truism of communal nudity in woods calls into question our own assumptions about its immorality.

'August', too, is right for trees, and, looked at in this unusual context, our restlessness *does* seem underbred:

> And common any taste for words;
> When, thoughtlessly, they took to song,
> Whatever one may think of birds,
> The example that they set was wrong

'Thoughtlessly', in keeping with the playful tone, means irresponsibly, but is also right for the evolutionary fact that it was not by choice but chance, so that the accusation of wrongness is seen as not to be taken seriously. The playfulness implies that these truths are not the whole truth. Meanwhile – before the theme of nature's superiority is given a twist – more genuine credit is given to trees. The image is conceptual, not perceptual, but it allows us to perceive clearly about trees qualities previously hardly realised at all:

> In keeping still, in staying slow,
> For posture and for social ease,
> How much these living statues owe
> Their scent-and-colour languages.

Trees cannot quarrel or invent irreconcilable differences:

> But trees are trees, an elm or oak
> Already both outside and in,
> And cannot, therefore, counsel folk
> Who have their unity to win.

Here the theme of personal integration is introduced. But is there not a hint that an inborn unity, though it may be enviable, is less valuable than one that has to be won? The next two stanzas appear to answer that question, though the masterly lucidity and ease of the style makes the witty paradoxes seem more self-evident than they are – at any rate to readers less clever than Auden:

> Turn all tree signals into speech,
> And what comes out is a command:
> 'Keep running if you want to reach
> The point of knowing where you stand.'
>
> A truth at which one should arrive,
> Forbids immediate utterance,
> And tongues to speak it must contrive
> To tell two different lies at once.

Trees, it would seem, set a good example only in terms of Being; their ambition is limited to knowing where they stand (which is where they have always stood); their running is always in the same direction (or, if you like, on the spot) and it gets them to where they already are. A message therefore not of much use to men, who are in a state of Becoming, whose truth is one to be arrived at, and will issue from conflict, a dialectic. Presumably the dialectic is between truths of the body and truths of the spirit – which are 'lies' in that neither is the whole truth.

The following stanza gives a further twist to the paradoxical idea of lying as a virtue:

> My chance of growing would be slim,
> Were I with wooden honesty
> To show my hand or heart to Him
> Who will, if I should lose, be Me.

One admires the wit with which trees are kept in mind by the overtones of 'growing' and 'wooden', but the idea behind 'Him' becoming 'Me' in a poker game seems at first utterly baffling. Perhaps the notions of art as a game that may by luck and grace reveal truth (truth from 'lie' again), and of the god-in-the-self, may help. Give up the game too soon, cease the dialectic, and one will cease to evolve. The god-in-oneself, seen as a principle of creativity in *The Sea and the Mirror*, would simply *be* the arrested self and cease to exist as a challenge to growth.

The final stanzas seem reasonably consistent with this inter-pretation.

> Our race would not have gotten far,
> Had we not learned to bluff it out
> And look more certain than we are
> Of what our motion is about;
>
> Nor need one be a cop to find
> Undressing before others rude:
> The most ascetic of our kind
> Look naked in the buff, not nude.

We seem to have come back to the beginning, with an excuse for human prudery; but by this time undressing surely has also the connotation of mental or spiritual exposure, and the 'motion' is that of inner becoming and not merely of changing place. The bluff, then, is part of the necessary dialectic of cross-fertilising lies that enables us to keep on growing towards an unattainable higher truth rather than settling with 'wooden honesty' for a lesser perfection. A teasingly humorous poem in which considerable complexity is mediated by a style of urbane simplicity.

Most of the themes mentioned earlier have now been dealt with – not thoroughly perhaps and often only in so far as they appeared in connection with other themes. It has appeared that the same kind of imagery – including the use of myth as a kind of imagery – may be used to embody different themes, and may occur in verse of very different kinds. This means that Auden's large output is rarely monotonous. Many of the same preoccupations may persist throughout his English and American periods, but since different combinations of theme occur in different poems, and imagery takes on a different colouring according to its context, the reader gets the aesthetic pleasure of variety within similarity.

What has not been adequately dealt with, even for a 'General' section, is the theme of trusting in something other than reason. The Absurd has, of course, cropped up in connection with other themes, but only as a form of inescapable contingency in reality, the fallen world; something to put up with, accept as a necessary evil.

For Kierkegaard, however, though it may be a source of anxiety or dread, it is something to be welcomed, as it makes the choice of faith 'pure' and 'authentic', untainted by rational or moral considerations, an act of will – and to will, utterly freely, is in his view the hallmark of true humanity.

'Leap Before You Look' is perhaps the poem that most clearly engages with this theme, uncomplicated by others: the theme of existential choice:

> The sense of danger must not disappear:
> The way is certainly both short and steep,
> However gradual it looks from here;
> Look if you like, but you will have to leap.
>
> Tough-minded men get mushy in their sleep
> And break the by-laws any fool can keep;
> It is not the convention but the fear
> That has a tendency to disappear.
>
> The worried efforts of the busy heap,
> The dirt, the imprecision, and the beer
> Produce a few smart wisecracks every year;
> Laugh if you can, but you will have to leap.
>
> The clothes that are considered right to wear
> Will not be either sensible or cheap,
> So long as we consent to live like sheep
> And never mention those who disappear.
>
> Much can be said for social savoir-faire,
> But to rejoice when no one else is there
> Is even harder than it is to weep;
> No one is watching, but you have to leap.
>
> A solitude ten thousand fathoms deep
> Sustains the bed on which we lie, my dear:
> Although I love you, you will have to leap;
> Our dream of safety has to disappear.
>> (*Collected Poems*, ed. Mendelson, p. 244)

Every stanza in effect rings the changes on the title. We start with a metaphor of height, end with one of depth. The first rhyme word and the last are 'disappear', and the message about danger and safety, is the same. From every point of view, it is implied, there is a requirement to trust the absurd, to leap before you look, rather than look before you leap as commonsense would have it. This implication is formally reinforced by the versification, since the stanzas run through every possible variation of the poem's two rhymes: abab, bbaa, baab, abba, aabb, baba.

Versification

More ought to be said of Auden's versification before this general section is concluded.

The sonnets of *In Time of War* alone would indicate Auden's marvellous command of verse technique. Though the sonnet form is normally used with great skill to point up the varied and fascinating arguments Auden regales us with as he runs through pre-human and human history, the reader also derives a purely aesthetic pleasure from the ease with which a difficult form and difficult ideas are so urbanely blended. Or beautifully varied: witness the way in which an easy disparagement of ideas as against harsh facts is avoided at the same time as the normal iambic pentameter of the sonnet form is twice suddenly shortened to make two telling points twice as telling:

> Here war is harmless like a monument:
> A telephone is talking to a man;
> Flags on a map declare that troops were sent;
> A boy brings milk in bowls. There is a plan
>
> For living men in terror of their lives,
> Who thirst at nine who were to thirst at noon,
> Who can be lost and are, who miss their wives
> And unlike an idea, can die too soon.
>
> Yet ideas can be true, although men die:
> For we have seen a myriad faces
> Ecstatic from one lie,
>
> And maps can really point to places
> Where life is evil now.
> Nanking. Dachau.
>
> (Op.cit. p. 153)

But later Auden achieves the extraordinary technical feat of writing a number of longish poems, full of ideas, in the idiom of casual intelligent conversation *in skaldic rhyme*: where each alternate line rhymes not with the ultimate but the penultimate syllable of the preceding line – as in these last four lines of 'Pleasure Island':

> Or hearing, beyond the hushabye noises
>   Of sea and Me, just a voice
> Ask, as one might the time or a trifle
>   Extra, her money and her life.
>   (Op.cit. p. 265)

This technique tends to take off the edge from content that could well have been bitingly satiric – a rather inappropriate mode for one holding Auden's later views. But it also contributes an aesthetic pleasure of its own, as jests, ideas, perceptions fountain forth and, without any straining of syntax or diction, constantly maintain this off-beat pattern.

Such pleasure in patterning imposed on sense instead of being organically inseparable from it was frowned upon by modernists (hence the contemporary preference for free verse), and Auden seems to have been influenced in his earlier work by that climate of opinion. Free verse is fairly rare, but so is the delight in difficult verse-forms. 'Night Mail' (op.cit. p. 113) may be taken as a nice example of early expertise. It was written in 1935 as a commentary to a G.P.O. publicity film (by John Grierson). Unusually, the pictures came first. Auden had to fit words not only to match the subject and the scenery but also the pace of the cutting – and a wholly admirable job he made of it. The train-rhythm is heard behind the lines, not too fast at first since the journey to the Border (*no* political implication here) is uphill:

> This is the Night Mail crossing the Border
> Bringing the cheque and the postal order,
> Letters for the rich, letters for the poor,
> The shop at the corner, the girl next door.
> Pulling up Beatock, a steady climb:
> The gradient's against her, but she's on time ...

On the downgrade towards Glasgow it speeds up, descending towards the 'furnaces/Set on the dark plain like gigantic chessmen' (one of a number of splendid images, equally apt and unexpected):

> Letters of thanks, letters from banks,
> Letters of joy from girl and boy,
> Receipted bills and invitations
> To inspect new stock or to visit relations,
> And applications for situations,
> And timid lovers' declarations,
> And gossip, gossip from all the nations ...

And finally it slows down as the train draws in:

> And none will hear the postman's knock
> Without a quickening of the heart.
> For who can bear to feel himself forgotten.

As the rhythm slows, the clattering rhyme disappears. Form too loses steam and quietens down.

'Nursery Rhyme' exemplifies a genuinely aesthetic use of varied repetition. Probably there is a mathematical basis to the form, for obviously the refrain-lines diverge as 123/321 and the rhyme-words always recur in a different place in the couplet, those that were first becoming second, those that were second becoming first, when they recur in another couplet. The point is, though, that one is not impelled to any further arithmetic. The verse form speaks for itself, endorsing

Night Mail

This is the night mail crossing the border,
Bringing the cheque and the postal order,
Letters for the rich, letters for the poor,
The shop at the corner and the girl next door.
Pulling up Beattock, a steady climb—
The gradient's against her but she's on time.
Past cotton grass and moorland boulder,
Shovelling white steam over her shoulder,
Snorting noisily as she passes
Silent miles of wind-bent grasses;
Birds turn their heads as she approaches,
Stare from the bushes at her blank-faced coaches;
Sheep dogs cannot turn her course,
They slumber on with paws across.
In the farm she passes no one wakes,
But a jug in the bedroom gently shakes.
Dawn freshens, the climb is done.
Down towards Glasgow she descends
Towards the steam tugs, yelping down the glade of cranes
Towards the fields of apparatus, the furnaces
Set on the dark plain like gigantic chessmen.
All Scotland waits for her;
In the dark glens, beside the pale-green sea lochs,
Men long for news.

The first half of Auden's commentary to a G.P.O. film
The leaflet was issued by the Post Office in 1938 to celebrate the centenary of
the Travelling Post Office

what appears to be the thematic content (which is also a wholly symbolic content, operating through what we have loosely styled mythic imagery). The idea seems to be that history repeats itself, but not so much in cycles as in a descending spiral – a theme counterpointed by the idea that there is a paradox in the nature of things: progress always has a heavy price-tag: the key that opens a sealed chamber being also the key that lets in a rusting process:

Their learned kings bent down to chat with frogs;
This was until the Battle of the Bogs.
The key that opens is the key that rusts.

Their cheerful kings made toffee on their stoves;
This was until the Rotting of the Loaves.
The robins vanish when the ravens come.

That was before the coaches reached the bogs;
Now woolly bears pursue the spotted dogs.
A witch can make an ogre out of mud.

That was before the weevils ate the loaves;
Now blinded bears invade the orange groves.
A witch can make an ogre out of mud.

The woolly bears have polished off the dogs;
Our bowls of milk are full of drowning frogs.
The robins vanish when the ravens come.

The blinded bears have rooted up the groves;
Our poisoned milk boils over on our stoves.
The key that opens is the key that rusts.

(*Collected Poems*, ed. Mendelson, p. 258)

Much more could be said about this neglected little poem, which is far more thought-provoking than its modest form and title ('Nursery Rhyme') suggest. Here, though, it is appropriate only to note that versification and other matters, such as theme, symbolism, and imagery, cannot long be kept separate – as a final, very different example of Auden's grasp and range of verse-form may confirm.

In Part Three of *New Year Letter* (op.cit. p. 181) Auden sets his face against both the metaphysical tendency to deny reality to the material world and to the converse tendency:

There are two atlases: the one
The public space where acts are done,
In theory common to us all,
Where we are needed and feel small

. . . .

The other is the inner space
Of private ownership, the place
That each of us is forced to own,
Like his own life from which it's grown

. . . .

Two worlds describing their rewards,
That one in tangents, this in chords;
Each lives in one, all in the other,
Here all are kings, there each a brother.

This might be seen as an extension of Auden's concern with conscious and unconscious worlds, political and private life, or the later body and spirit relationship. At any rate, much of Auden's poetry can be read as a series of attempts to build up three-dimensional models of places in one or the other of these atlases, or to test them for compatibility. What is notable here, and relevant to our present concern, is the one-dimensionality of the statement. Even more than in the case of 'Aubade' (discussed on p. 69) the verse itself forms an essential part of the imagery. Structurally, the piece is divided into three parts: one for each atlas and one to compare and contrast. The neat couplet form reinforces the clarity of idea as each line contributes its row of metrical bricks towards the arch of argument – a neatness perfectly in keeping with the balances of public space and private place, of all and each, social and personal. This is most apparent in the last part; the geometrical image of tangents and chords certainly does not give body to the argument. On the contrary, like the other images (but more so), it keeps body at bay for the sake of utter lucidity of understanding. A very necessary lucidity, for the final couplet is to give a twist in the tail by showing that these radically different worlds are also indissolubly united. If each lives in one world and all live in the other (and this hardly seems disputable) then logically all the 'ones' must be contained in the 'other', and we must go on to accept the paradox that every man is at once a king and an equal. A difference-in-unity that the verse-form positively helps to establish, since it matches the sense in being both divisive and uniting. Each line is a world to itself, metrically complete and end-stopped, each is further divided by antithesis (the two halves of each line being mutually exclusive); yet the crossing of chiasmus in the couplet as a whole (not to mention the linkage of rhyme) unites the worlds. But the 'each' of the first line is logically the 'all' of the second, while the verbally similar 'each' of the second is logically the 'all' of the first. Thus a sort of verbal confusion oddly supports a precise logic, and antithesis and chiasmus (itself a form of antithesis) play against each other but as a team. Even more oddly, it seems unlikely that a prose statement could have conveyed so complex a case with the clarity of this verse.

This poetry happens to be exceptionally expository; its *raison d'être* is to tease out an idea. First it distinguishes two strands of existence, of 'the baffle of being', and then shows that they are knotted together. Even so, it finds it necessary, so to speak, to colour them for clarity's sake. To do so, it calls imagery and verse into play, and they become an inseparable part of the points being made.

In most poetry, even of Auden's, exposition plays a considerably smaller part; a poem is normally less a statement than an ongoing verbal experience; so an appreciation of it rarely, if ever, consists in arriving at an opinion. Nor does it consist even in a literary total arrived at by adding together various elements and aspects after analysis, though this would be nearer to the truth. A truly literary appreciation is not so much a *product* of critical reading – or, more often, re-reading – as the *process* of it. So all background information about the writer, his times, his environment, and his beliefs, all separation of aspects of his verse, is valuable only in so far as it leads ultimately to the informed enjoyment of particular poems as they are being read.

No kind of critical analysis can completely avoid separation: that is the nature of the beast. At best, it is a signpost for the reader, not a destination. However, the two following sections, in that they treat a selection of poems as unique wholes, may serve as a partial corrective to much that has gone before as well as being a conclusion to this critical survey.

From this point the poems chosen for discussion are taken from Mendelson's *Selected Poems*, with page-references to the *Collected Poems*, where Auden's final revisions sometimes include the addition of an ironic or mocking title.

5 Poems of the 'English' Period

If Auden tends at times to be hectoring in the English period and unctuous in the American the tendency is modified as we have seen, by his habit of associating political or religious themes with those of Nature, Art, or Society. Even more are they modified by his habit of mythicising; and most of all by the subversive activities of the Antipoet. If Auden tends to abstract and conceptualise, to see a generalisation within particulars, the tendency is modified by his sharp eye for details that are striking as well as significant, by his lyrical gift, and his ability to present ideas in the form of little allegories or dramas (the operative word being 'little'; the long allegories despite their brilliances tend to become tedious, and the plays – since he had no gift for characterisation – are inferior to other expressions of his themes). Even the most entertaining conversationalist turns into a bore if he holds forth too long.

The earliest poems, especially, startle the reader out of his normal perceptions by syntactical disturbances, derived from Hopkins, Pound and Eliot, but pay a fairly heavy price in terms of obscurity. However, even obscure poems are usually concerned with definite ideas; they may be eccentric but are not irrational on principle in the modernist way. Auden's confessed difficulty with punctuation, and his habit of saving good lines from scrapped poems to work into later compositions, also flaw the earliest poetry. After 1935, however, most of this disappears. Obscurity, where it occurs, is more likely to be the result of a proper awareness of the actual complexity – due to liberalism, traditionalism, and pacificism – beneath the simplicity of the Left/Right polarity supposed to typify the Thirties. Or it is likely to be the result of a proper awareness of the actual complexity of feeling even in the most committed mind.

In any case, Auden's belief in the value of light verse pushed him towards the linguistic clarity that is typical of much of the later 'English' poetry as well as most of the 'American'. His Introduction to the *Oxford Book of Light Verse*, 1938, defines it as that in which author and audience are on the same wavelength and in which the language is straightforward and normal. Such verse was to include not only parody – a frequent characteristic of the Antipoet's intrusions – but also, more surprisingly, nonsense. Much that is attributed to the influence of surrealism (of which Auden has spoken reprovingly) is surely owed to more traditional kinds of nonsense. At any rate that certainly seems to be true of the first of our samples, since its dream images are clearly selected and organised so as to make a point. In short, it is relatively sensible nonsense – whose exuberance, as so often in Auden's Thirties' work, even in serious poems, is in tension with sombre implications in the content.

O for doors to be open

O for doors to be open and an invite with gilded edges
To dine with Lord Lobcock and Count Asthma on the platinum
   benches,
With the somersaults and fireworks, the roast and the smacking kisses –
     Cried the six cripples to the silent statue,
     The six beggared cripples.

And Garbo's and Cleopatra's wits to go astraying,
In a feather ocean with me to go fishing and playing
Still jolly when the cock has burst himself with crowing –
     Cried the six cripples to the silent statue,
     The six beggared cripples.

And to stand on green turf among the craning yellow faces,
Dependent on the chestnut, the sable, and Arabian horses,
And me with a magic crystal to foresee their places –
     Cried the six cripples to the silent statue,
     The six beggared cripples.

And this square to be a deck, and these pigeons sails to rig
And to follow the delicious breeze like a tantony pig
To the shaded feverless islands where the melons are big –
     Cried the six cripples to the silent statue,
     The six beggared cripples.

And these shops to be turned to tulips in a garden bed,
And me with my stick to thrash each merchant dead
As he pokes from a flower his bald and wicked head –
     Cried the six cripples to the silent statue,
     The six beggared cripples.

And a hole in the bottom of heaven, and Peter and Paul
And each smug surprised saint like parachutes to fall,
And every one-legged beggar to have no legs at all –
     Cried the six cripples to the silent statue,
     The six beggared cripples. (1935)
      (*W. H. Auden: Selected Poems*, ed. Mendelson, 1979, p. 42.
                     Collected Poems, p. 116)

At first sight, a poem that defines itself negatively: it is not obviously Freudian or Marxist, nor is it obviously thematic or didactic. Indeed it

is obviously not didactic at all. However, poems may express themes
without being didactic, in that they can be implied by the content
without being explicitly asserted. And there are indications that this is
such a poem. The very fact that it is not *obviously* Freudian or Marxist is
one, for on further consideration there does seem to be a touch of
Freud and Marx. After all, it is rather like a dream, in so far as it is
crammed with images of wish-fulfilment, and Marx might have found
the juxtaposition of beggars with members of the nobility and the
bourgeoisie significant of the class-structure. On the other hand, the
dream-images are not as disguised and distorted as in real dreams, and
the class conflict is not taken seriously. Indeed – again at first sight – it
is tempting to take it as straightforward farce (laughter for its own
sake). But on consideration, again, there seems to be more to it than
that. Surely, it is comedy that looks like farce because its matter looks
like nonsense?

John Fuller says that it is a poem about the Freudian idea of art as
wish-fulfilment or compensation – to which the only appropriate
critical response seems to be 'Oh, yeah?' Admittedly, the beggared
cripples might be said to be creating little works of art, a series of
fantastical vignettes. But at most that would indicate only that the
poem contained *examples* of art as compensation, not that it was *about*
that. Much more obviously the latent, or implied, theme is political;
and the mode of comedy what we might call *mithridatic* (the sort that
vaccinates us against despair, lets us laugh in order not to weep).

The poem's kind is that of a street ballad; it is characterised, as they
often were, by sprung rhythm rather than metre (four main stresses to
the line, two in the refrain-lines), and by rather loose grammar – e.g.
'invite' and the 'withs' of lines 2 and 3. A deliberate pastiche; the style
is roughly appropriate to the beggars who are supposed to be speaking
(or rather singing, as this is a ballad). Such ballads commonly
expressed the common man's feeling about his unfortunate lot, as
compared with that of Them, and very often they disguised satire in
fantasy. This poem is clearly not *about* escapism (any more than it is
about art); it is an *example* of escapism (and of popular art). An
example that does seem to have a point, and therefore to be comic in
the strict sense, though it uses a method common to farce. What is the
point? Surely that it is a sick society which allows some to live in
absurd luxury while others have nothing but envious dreams of it – a
point Auden makes seriously in the preceding poem (No. 25):

> Just and unjust, worst and best,
> Change their places as they rest . . .

In addition to social concern – mediated in the Antipoet's clowning
manner – we may also detect a hint of the Failed-Quest theme, for the
unholy grail of an 'invite with gilded edges' will never be achieved.
And is there not also something of Audenesque mythicising, in that

certain aspects of society are expressed by fictionalised stereotypes? Stereotypes, perhaps, of gargantuan feasting, fornicating, fortune-making, gallivanting, and turning the tables, in that order. To put it another way, we have six vignettes, each item being a pop-art logo for a whole section of society.

Auden, then, is following – as he so often did – the method Ford and Conrad advocated for the novel; that of the exhaustion of aspects. Indeed, on close reading, the individual items themselves reveal several aspects; in short, are no more real stereotypes than pop-paintings are real posters. The scenes of the first four stanzas – which express positive wishes – are, respectively, banqueting hall, bed, racecourse, and yacht, and the elements mentioned are certainly shown as being present in these places; whether they are *dominant* is another matter.

In the first stanza, for instance, prestige seems to be more important than feasting. The company and the open entry, the gilding and the platinum, seem to outweigh the roast. The main speech-stresses, too, fall on the first syllables of Lobcock, Asthma, platinum and benches, not on 'dine'. In stanza two, the glamour of Garbo and Cleopatra seems at least as important as the sex-fantasy. So too the lust for money, which is the ostensible point of the third stanza, seems subordinated to the desire for translation to an aesthetic environment, to being part of a colourful picture (or more likely, a sporting-print – which could account realistically for the yellow faces that so pleasingly accompany the patches of green, sable, and chestnut). And in the fourth stanza the physical pleasures envisaged are surely minor compared with the general idea of enjoying the fashionable *dolce vita*. The last two stanzas form a structural contrast, since they express negative fantasies of revengeful envy and anti-clerical contempt. Yet they too are not simple expressions of such feelings, for there is something jocular and elfin in the snapshot of the merchant's bald head poking from a flower, which takes all the sting from 'wicked'. In the same way, the picture of the saints floating down, frocks billowing about them, cancels some of the connotations of 'smug'.

All this, however, is far from all there is. In particular, we might say that though there is little verisimilitude in this poem there is a good deal of realism. There is little verisimilitude because the scenes are garishly exaggerated (who sits on platinum benches? Who would want to?). It is as if Auden were taking the allegorical cliché of the world as Vanity Fair almost literally. Moreover, even in the grim Thirties cripples did not have to beg in the public squares. These seem more akin to the traditional professional beggars of earlier centuries (and their vision of the feasts of the aristocracy seems much more like the revel of Burns's roistering *Jolly Beggars* than of any actual upper-class banquet). The poem could be styled realistic, on the other hand, because the desires are far from noble and selfless (these are no social reformers), are recognised to be jovial fantasies, and are corrected by a seasoning of cynicism. Thus Lord Lobcock and Count Asthma – cases of weakness at each end – not only seem to symbolise a sick society, but to be less capable of enjoyment than the beggars. (Partridge's *Dictionary of Historical Slang* defines 'Lobcock' as 'a blockhead; a large relaxed *membrum virile*' – in modern slang he is a stupid, useless prick.) It is recognised that Garbo and Cleopatra would have to go out of their minds to allow a beggared cripple to bed them, let alone be still 'jolly' at dawn (and presumably, if we see the same pun here as in stanza one, when the beggars have done what poor Lobcock is incapable of). The very elegance of the next stanza acknowledges its fantasy, and the fantasy of the remaining stanzas is undercut by the farcical touches of the tantony pig, the 'flower' merchants and the 'parachute' saints.

The last wish of all carries this chiaroscuro of moods to an extreme: 'And every one-legged beggar to have no legs at all' suggesting at once the bitter blessing, for a professional beggar, of being exceptionally crippled and an ironic acknowledgement that further disaster is a more likely eventuality than the realisation of those dreams.

Throughout, then, the rough ride of the rhythm is matched by a switchback of feelings: a fairground ride with only a symbolic relation to life (much as was Pabst's film of the *Threepenny Opera* (1930), with its great sequence of the revolt of the beggars – a film almost certain to have been seen by Auden). This careful distance from reality, without losing touch with it, is maintained by period slang ('lobcock'), and period detail (a featherbed, giving a wallowing sexual experience – implied by 'ocean' – as against the more hygienic resilience of the modern sprung-mattress), and above all by the out-of-date scene of a gang of cripples begging in the public square. What, now, does the refrain add to make up the total of a poem that has turned out to have so much more to it than appeared at first sight?

These lines are shorter than the rest, they don't rhyme, and they reiterate one aspect – whatever it is – instead of proceeding over several. Their tone, too, suggests the mood of a minor key in contrast to the major of the verses; it is decidedly unroistering, unboisterous. This is largely due to the presence of the 'silent' statue. Perhaps here we do have a slight surrealist influence. Chirico was in vogue during the Thirties; his empty squares and brooding giant statues struck a contemporary chord. At any rate, the statue here suggests a dead god. Naturally it is unresponsive to the prayer of the beggared cripples ('O for an invite . . .') since it has a heart of stone – like the reality they are temporarily almost escaping from, perhaps. Certainly, as statues in public squares are usually larger than lifesize, famous, and idealised in physique, it emphasises by contrast their deprivation and distortion, and is a standing reproof to the vigorous vulgarity of their dreams. If, at some level (as seems to be the case in the Pabst/Brecht

Dreigroschenoper) the beggars represent not only the underworld of society but that of the individual, the Id, then the statue seems to stand for all that might be related to the holier-than-thou Superego.

Look, stranger

Look, stranger, at this island now
The leaping light for your delight discovers,
Stand stable here
And silent be,
That through the channels of the ear
May wander like a river
The swaying sound of the sea.

Here at the small field's ending pause
Where the chalk wall falls to the foam, and its tall ledges
Oppose the pluck
And knock of the tide,
And the shingle scrambles after the suck-
ing surf, and the gull lodges
A moment on its sheer side.

Far off like floating seeds the ships
Diverge on urgent voluntary errands;
And the full view
Indeed may enter
And move in memory as now these clouds do,
That pass the harbour mirror
And all the summer through the water saunter.   (1935)
                   (*Selected Poems*, p. 43. *Collected Poems*, p. 112)

The poem seems to start with the idea of being didactic, like 'Consider', and end in being almost romantic. Lyrical it certainly is, as a whole, for the public voice of the opening soon dissolves into the sort of musing that we think of as particularly characteristic of lyric: verse that is not so much listened to as overheard. Yet there is no sense of incongruity or changing mind in midstream; despite the variation of tone, it is all of a piece, as organic a poem as, say, Keats's ode 'To Autumn'. An explanation of this blended unity may lie in the word 'stranger'. Who is he? Can he really be a foreigner, taken to the cliffs of Dover and exhorted to admire England? Surely not; a persona so insensitive would hardly be capable of the inward, musing beauty of the last stanza. Perhaps it is simply the reader, invited to witness a transformation scene; for the first two lines do suggest the spotlights of a theatre, and the dis-covering rising of the curtain, almost as much as they suggest dawn. There's a sense of a show being put on, 'for your delight'. A little of this does seem implicit. But we have not got the metaphor quite right yet. More accurately, surely, the reader is being asked *to share a revelation*. Share? Must not that mean that the poet (or persona) is a stranger also? Yet he seems to have a remarkable command of the English language, and to be already familiar with the land the light 'now' discovers. The same things seem to be assumed, too, of the reader. On the other side of the question, though, is the fact that this idea of sharing would account for the blend of public and private voice. And if the poet were taking himself to be a representative *native* 'stranger' speaking to and for other native strangers it would be natural enough for the two voices to blend rather than clash. So is there some sense of 'stranger' that will by-pass the objections raised above?

That hint of didacticism in the opening line may well be our clue. 'Look, stranger . . .'. It's as if some quester had arrived at his destination without knowing it, and was witnessing his begging bowl being transformed into the Holy Grail. If we remember that the quest was almost always more psychological than physical (though often both), then our assumption seems quite possible. If we remember too Auden's fondness for paradox, it becomes highly probable. It would be quite in keeping for Auden to cast himself and the sort of people who read his poems as strangers: both to themselves, and within their own land. Nor would such 'alienation' be out of keeping with his Marxism.

This is not to suggest that the poem is predominantly assertive or thematic. On the contrary, it exists far more as a hum of reverberations than a structure of statements, even metaphorical ones. It is a genuine lyric in that sense too. But little bits of Auden's preoccupations seem to be scattered in it, rather like the 'floating seeds' of his ships. For one thing we are at a *border*, between two worlds in space, those of land and sea; between two seasons, of summer and, the last stanza implies, winter; and between the physical and the mental: we start with light and end with enlightenment ('the full view'), or, looking becomes memorable vision. *Time, dualism*, and *body/spirit* are also obviously latently there (witness: the passing of summer, and 'now', which implies a previous unenlightened view; 'stable' and 'swaying', or the cliffs opposing the tide; and the intangible 'clouds' in the physical mirror of the harbour, like memories or ideas in the brain, at once physical and meta-physical). But more fructifying than these is the *quest*-seed. Little more needs to be given than the hint in 'stranger', 'floating seeds' (which will one day arrive, root, and flower) and the '*full* view'. For this seems to be an expression of the Successful Quest, the partial view having passed into the full view, opposed elements having been harmonised in a balanced delight, and the 'stranger' come home to himself and his land – for the moment, as the gull lodges a moment.

The surrealist influence of de Chirico – Gare Montparnasse (The Melancholy of Departure)

114

Again, this is not so much a poem about achieved integration as an example of it. Theme is almost entirely absorbed into subject, symbolism into naturalism. Various minor harmonies imperceptibly build up to a harmonious whole in which potentially separative elements are integrated. Thus the border here is not a barrier but a meeting place, where the estranged persona and reader perceive both land and sea in a new light, where one stands stable to be aware of swaying, where silence and sound become interdependent – as indeed water and land, humanity and nature are seen to be in the image that involves the 'channels' of the ear, a river, and the sea. In the second stanza too the opposition of cliff and tide seems more in the nature of a match than a battle. The almost comic idea of the shingle scrambling after the surf, too, is in keeping with the sense of a game. The gull too, though as different from the cliff as mind from muscle, is in precarious harmony with it. The man-made and the natural are blended in the image of ships as floating seeds; as seeds and sea blend the life-giving and the deadly. And finally, the last lines merge man and nature, present, future, and past, tangible (the mirror) and intangible (the image in it) in a compound harmony.

That this harmony is not simply external and naturalistic is indicated by a number of tips in the poem. We do not need to deduce it from Auden's symbolising and internalising habits elsewhere. Most clearly, of course, internalising is indicated by 'enter' in the last stanza. Equally clearly '*as* now these clouds do', indicates that the 'full view' that will move in memory is something other than (though comparable to) a merely visual memory of a purely physical harmony. But internalising has been delicately suggested in the first stanza's 'stand stable'. How else would one stand, unless drunk? Mental or emotional stability is inevitably evoked. In this context, the 'pause' where everything meets and matches also inevitably takes on a symbolic overtone.

So far we have concentrated on the poem's semantics, but the semantic meaning is remarkably reinforced by sound-effects. In this short lyric are to be found no fewer than thirty-one sibilants (s and z sounds) and forty-six fricatives (f, v, sh, and th sounds): precisely the sounds that Tennyson took pains to eliminate. 'Kicking the geese out of the boat', he called this practice. Why has Auden not followed his admirable advice? Surely because in this particular case a background susurrus merging finally into a murmur of *m*'s is wholly appropriate – a sonic equivalent to the distant visual perception of the sea from a cliff top. There are also twenty-six labials which – again, *in conjunction with the semantic sense* – reinforce the feeling of almost aerial buoyancy in the work. These sounds, as it were, form a structure of sound-sinews round the skeletal semantic structure.

Sonic effects, however, are also deeply interwoven into the *texture* of this poem, in many ways. For one thing there is an aesthetically pleasing system of echoes, almost independent of sense – though not quite, since it supports the general suggestion of achieved integration, of discords resolved in harmony. Witness, in the first stanza alone, the interplay of 'l', 'd', 'ee' and 'i' sounds in the second line, the assonances and consonances (or approximations) of *str*anger, *st*and, and *st*able, of *isl*- and *sil*- and *-els*, of *-land* and *wand-*. When we come to *sta-* and *sway-*, of course, we are passing into the area of textural interdependence of sound and sense, as these two words take part in rendering the paradox of harmony. We are still and silent to absorb swaying and sound; and all four items become part of one inner-and-outer experience. Similarly, after 'pause' we *do* pause, having come to the end of a line and a clause as well as the end of the land. Ch*alk*, w*all*, f*all*, and t*all*, too, sonically enact the sense of 'sheer side'. The sound effects of *pluck*, *knock*, and *suck*-ing (the last word clearly *not* broken merely to get a rhyme) are perhaps too obvious to be worth mentioning. But the change of metre from iambics to anapaests in the 'shingle-scrambling' line exemplifies a more subtle sound-effect, for the voice has to hurry to get the extra syllables in (a four-foot iambic line's rhyme would chime easily with the two-foot iambic line ending in 'pluck', but we are not given four iambs). The concluding lines of the poem – in every sense of the word – speak, and speak beautifully, for themselves. Like the harbour, they mirror a moving harmony.

Does 'moving' seem ominously ambiguous? Are we left with the feeling not only that such a state of balance and reconciliation needs constant adjustment, comparable to that of a gull, but also that it will gradually move away, become less potent, as talismanic memories do in time? Surely we are. The 'now' of the first stanza, reiterated in the last, hints at the temporary, as does 'summer' and 'memory'. Moreover, 'urgent' seems not quite at home with 'voluntary' and is certainly at odds with 'saunter'. And it is at this point, at any rate if one is aware of the international situation, that the clouds are seen, so to speak, also to cast a shadow. Why are these ships, life-giving traders, on *urgent* voluntary errands? In some sense, no doubt, all commercial enterprises have a degree of urgency. But that goes without saying. The fact that it *is* said suggests a fear that they must make haste while the going is still good; that soon the urgent errands will be compulsory, and many of the ships more like bullets than seeds. And thus the 'full view' becomes a little fuller, a little less delighted and enlightened than the main drift of the poem implies. Into the late summer harmony is infiltrated an autumnal tinge.

In Time of War (XIX)

> But in the evening the oppression lifted;
> The peaks came into focus; it had rained:
> Across the lawns and cultured flowers drifted

The conversation of the highly trained.

The gardeners watched them pass and priced their shoes;
A chauffeur waited, reading in the drive,
For them to finish their exchange of views;
It seemed a picture of the private life.

Far off, no matter what good they intended,
The armies waited for a verbal error
With all the instruments for causing pain:

And on the issue of their charm depended
A land laid waste, with all its young men slain,
The women weeping, and the towns in terror.   (1938)
                          (*Selected Poems*, p. 74. *Collected Poems*, p. 155)

At first sight, the most obvious thing to be said of this sonnet is that little needs to be said. Already Auden seems to have graduated into the lucid suavity of his later period; sense and syntax alike seem perfectly clear, no suspect philosophy or propagandist politics flaw the clinical compassion of its contemplation – a contemplation that attempts to move from sight to insight, from scene to scenario. It is a regular Petrarchan sonnet in that it divides into an octet (or octave), grounded in local detail, and a sestet brooding on its significance. It is mildly irregular, however, in that the octet follows the rhyme-scheme of a Shakespearian sonnet: a tactful reminder, perhaps, that the content is very different from that traditionally associated with either Petrarchan or Shakespearian sonnets.

One reason for the pellucid surface is that nothing is taken to excess. Gone is alliteration as a principle of structure, on the Anglo-Saxon model, or as a regular support for sense (as in 'Look, stranger'). Here it operates unobtrusively to add a further feeling of structuring to that more obviously provided by the rhyme and metre. This parallels the effort to get the subject matter into order, 'into focus'. Here and there, too, it seems to condense what might have been dissipated in detail into an almost proverbial succinctness: 'a picture of the private life', 'A land laid waste ... the women weeping'.

Another reason is the absence of imagery, of metaphors and other figures of speech; what we have instead are significant details, telling instances. Auden's mastery of both modes has already been commented on; the latter, though, is the more specifically his; most poets rely almost exclusively on imagery. Certainly, imagery enriches a poem by assimilating areas of reference, emotional or material, that would normally lie outside the realm of the primary sense. The risk is that the reader may feel that he is being manipulated, and while he won't mind this in poems that purport to convey a verbal *experience*, he quite properly may if it is rather a *truth* or a considered *opinion* that is being conveyed. In these latter cases – fairly common in Auden –

reliance on significant detail comes into its own; what the poem loses in richness and overtone, it gains in clarity and validity.

But what are these details, and how do they work? The first example comes in the opening line. Granted that the general heading to the sonnet-sequence is 'In Time of War' and that we know it to refer to the Japanese invasion of China, then the 'oppression' becomes a detail about the weather that also reminds us of the war and its effect on the people; its lifting being comparable to the lull ('the armies waited') that is permitting negotiations. It also suggests that they are as uncertain as the weather. In this context, 'the peaks' seem equivalent to crucial issues that have become evident in the course of a general 'clearing of the air'. The 'cultured' flowers hint at the difference between what is civilised, trained, and cared for, and the 'wildness' without, between the worlds of war and peace, militarists and diplomats. The association with civilisation and diplomacy is reinforced by 'drifted', a word suggestive of scent or pollen or mist. But is there not also a warning hint of artificiality and vulnerability, a precarious remoteness from the unprotected, unprivileged world? It has ceased to rain, but that 'drift' could just as well be mist as pollen; the poem is tinged with foreboding from the start.

The remoteness of the two worlds is emphasised in the second quatrain, since the gardeners and the chauffeur have no idea of the issues and the dangers. To them 'It seemed a picture of the private life'. This seems to hint, too, at the vast distances of China – a hint picked up by 'Far off'. It also points to the distance between classes that was to result in the triumph of communism – a point strengthened in the revised version of the sonnet by the alteration of 'The gardeners' to 'Thin gardeners'. Implicitly, in these quatrains, the trivial is set against the immense – a relationship made explicit in the sestet.

> 'Far off, no matter what they intended,
> The armies waited for a verbal error'

The 'they' is slightly ambiguous. It links the two sections by picking up the preceding 'their' and thus refers primarily to the diplomats. The armies then are seen as waiting, and wanting, to fulfil their role of wreaking havoc – unlike the chauffeur, who is waiting in innocent ignorance. However, as the 'they' comes in the same sentence, it could momentarily seem to refer to armies, which would then simply be poised, liable to be toppled into combat even if they might have intended an armistice. The former meaning seems to predominate, especially in view of the bitter wit of 'instruments', which underlines the fact that a soldier is the reverse of a doctor: dedicated to killing, not curing, to causing rather than relieving pain.

In either case, there is an anticipation of a theme that was to feature more in the American period: the idea of contingency – for what could be more 'absurd' than the dependence of widespread horror in one place on charm and verbal art in another? Clearly, if faintly, then, the theme of art and reality, of the structuring effort needed to civilise incipient chaos, is also present. We can add the sub-theme (subsumable under that of the 'Absurd') of ordinary life going on, necessarily and unawares, side by side with events of magnitude – a theme prominent in 'Musée des Beaux Arts', but here largely restricted to the second quatrain. And, of course, the sonnet as a whole exemplifies Auden's typical striving for 'the full view', the attempt to combine the particular with the panoramic.

As a footnote, it is worth looking at the small, and purely technical revisions Auden made. The metre of the first line is made more regular by changing the first five words to 'As evening fell the day's . . .'. The change also gives us a balance (of night and day) that is appropriate in view of the larger balances of war and peace, local and large, lower and upper class, charm and terror, culture and wildness, order and chaos already noted. Realistically speaking, too, it bolsters the idea that 'oppression' should suggest more than thundery weather, for hostilities normally cease at night. 'The peaks' become 'Tall peaks'. This avoids the suggestion that we should know where we are and that the area contains peaks, and perhaps gives a little more support to the symbolic hint of *crucial* issues. It indicates, too, that the oppression has lifted very considerably; so that the 'climate' is right for talks. The change to '*Thin* gardeners' has already been mentioned. In the last line of the sonnet two more rather inert definite articles are eliminated, this time in favour of 'its' – a change that at least allows grammar not to blur, however slightly, the cumulative effect of the semantic pile-up that concludes the poem. All these changes, slight though they are, seem to be improvements – and significantly, improvements that self-effacingly direct attention to the sense rather than to sensational stylistic effects.

Lay your sleeping head

Lay your sleeping head, my love,
Human on my faithless arm;
Time and fevers burn away
Individual beauty from
Thoughtful children, and the grave
Proves the child ephemeral:
But in my arms till break of day
Let the living creature lie,
Mortal, guilty, but to me
The entirely beautiful.

Soul and body have no bounds:
To lovers as they lie upon
Her tolerant enchanted slope

In their ordinary swoon,
Grave the vision Venus sends
Of supernatural sympathy,
Universal love and hope;
While an abstract insight wakes
Among the glaciers and the rocks
The hermit's sensual ecstasy.

Certainty, fidelity
On the stroke of midnight pass
Like vibrations of a bell,
And fashionable madmen raise
Their pedantic boring cry:
Every farthing of the cost,
All the dreaded cards foretell,
Shall be paid, but from this night
Not a whisper, not a thought,
Not a kiss nor look be lost.

Beauty, midnight, vision dies:
Let the winds of dawn that blow
Softly round your dreaming head
Such a day of sweetness show
Eye and knocking heart may bless,
Find the mortal world enough;
Noons of dryness see you fed
By the involuntary powers,
Nights of insult let you pass
Watched by every human love.   (1937)
(*Selected Poems*, p. 50. *Collected Poems*, p. 133)

For a change, a poem of the Thirties that has nothing whatever to do with politics; an 'island' poem of the private life; in short, a personal love-lyric. Hardly, however, an orthodox traditional one. Such lyrics do not begin, as this does, with what amounts to a tender acceptance of mutual infidelity. Almost invariably, too, they attempt to reflect the experience of love, whereas this – typically Audenesque – reflects upon it. Indeed, the proportion of explored ideas to expressed feelings is high enough to suggest that though it *is* finally a lyric poem it is one that lies near to the border of narrative poetry – the poetry one listens to or attends to rather than overhears and shares. In keeping with this propensity for meditation, both metre and rhyme are muted. The irregular trochaics, assimilated to the rhythms of inner speech, the many run-on lines, and the half-rhyme contrast strongly with the formal assertiveness of the traditional love-lyric, in which regular metre and full rhyme usually match a highly-charged rhetoric. Here a moderated formality matches a meditated emotion.

Does a combination of form and informality sound almost a contradiction in terms? Perhaps – but then so is a philosophic love-lyric, which is what this seems to be. The theme of the poem, in the sense of message or thesis, is traditional enough: love now, pay later – whatever the cost it will still have been worthwhile. But the separate stanzas bring in four themes (in the sense of preoccupations) that so diffuse the first as to render the poem as a whole distinctly original and modern. In the first stanza we have Time as the enemy, but here without any political reference; in the second, man's duality, seen in terms of soul and body; in the third, an anticipation of existentialism's insistence on willed free choice rather than inert acceptance of convention – an early hint for 'Leap Before You Look'; and in the fourth, the assumption of sex, *per se*, as a good. Freud's influence is pervasive, but most evident in the second and fourth stanzas. All this tends to remove the poem from the simplicity usually associated with lyrics – an inheritance from their origin in song; so a line by line explanatory critique – even at the risk of 'hunting down the obvious with all the enthusiasm of a shortsighted detective' (Oscar Wilde) – may be the best mode of procedure from here.

The poem starts with a dramatically rendered cameo, of lovers in a *post*-erotic situation favourable to ambling meditation. 'Human' clearly means fallible (cp 'Mortal, guilty') but also seems designed to keep out traditional admixtures of divinity or religion. 'Faithless', which is self-accusing, eliminates any holier-than-thou implication. The scene is set – and suddenly we move away from it, into a meditation on Time. Yet this seems natural enough; probably because a sleeping face relaxes and smooths out, thus bringing to mind the unlined faces of children and therefore the passage of Time. All the same there is something odd about these lines. What time and fevers (presumably life's passions) really seem to do to the bland faces of childhood is to burn *in* lines, which make the face more, not less, individual. It is even arguable whether the process burns away, or creates, beauty – at any rate until it reaches a rather advanced stage. Possibly Auden means that time burns away the beauty of *each* individual. If so, the meaning is not well expressed. However one takes them, these lines seem to constitute one of the few flaws in a fine poem. Another may lie in the fact that it does seem a little extravagant – almost medieval – to say that death proves the child *ephemeral*. True, childhood doesn't last long; but neither does it end in death. Moreover the 'But . . .' of the next line confirms that we are speaking of the child's life – i.e. anyone's life. So the line simply seems to create a lament for brevity out of the truism that we must all die one day. One wonders if 'grave' wasn't prompted by an unconscious association with 'thoughtful'! After the colon, the mode of address changes to one of self-communing – a communion, however, that moves away from 'my love' to the more generalised 'living creature', and goes on to admit –

an admission that is also a claim – that the judgement 'entirely beautiful' is merely personal. In the light of 'Mortal, guilty', 'entirely' must paradoxically mean *morally* as well as physically, or the 'but' would have no relevance. The stanza, then, tacitly acknowledges a certain element of illusion, as well as temporariness and imperfection, in their love – and through the generalising effect of 'living creature' hints that this is characteristic of human love. The second stanza (along with the third, and the first line of the fourth) continues to move outwards, leaving the particular love affair behind.

'Soul and body have no bounds:' sounds like a traditional highfaluting assertion of their boundlessness, but the punctuation of the stanza alone is sufficient to indicate that what is being said is that there is no definable boundary between them: man is a psychosomatic unity, as Freud, Groddeck and Homer Lane had taught. Lovers are shown to move from the physical – culminating in an orgasmic 'swoon' which the Antipoet describes as 'ordinary' – to the spiritual. On the other hand, the hermit, starting from an 'abstract insight' into the supernatural, and universal love and hope, ends in accordance with Freudian theory, in what is essentially a sensual ecstasy. Something of the initial misapprehension of 'Soul and body have no bounds', however, seems to linger in the mind. It may be an illusion, as 'enchanted' and 'vision' hint, but it is not a worthless one; and indeed the words are favourably qualified by 'tolerant' and 'Grave'. So the final result is far from being dismissive or debunking.

The idea of a worthwhile illusion is picked up in the next stanza by the oblique reference to the Cinderella legend which opens it. Just as her finery turned back to rags on the stroke of midnight, so certainty and fidelity, at some crisis, will pass – a point latent, of course, in the second line of the poem. 'Fashionable madmen' is presumably Auden's flippant way of referring to, and undermining, those bishops and other publicly-approved moral pontificators opposed to sexual permissiveness. After the colon we get their words, as imagined by the poet, who agrees, so to speak, that there'll be hell to pay, but then goes on to show he doesn't give a damn.

The poem ends by acknowledging that the physical and spiritual beauty of love, its enchanted eroticism, its ennobling visions are all subject to time, but claims, in the remaining lines of the stanza (which move back to direct address) that they leave a sort of underground reservoir that may provide salvation in time of drought. The 'mortal world' refers us back to the 'mortal' of the first stanza, with its implications both of 'fallible' and 'secular' – implications reinforced by the 'human' of the last line, which rounds off the poem by taking us back to the same word at the beginning.

A prayer, whether secular or religious, is not an assertion of fact but a request or even a wish; so it need not be examined too strictly. Still, it is tempting to ask just what is meant by 'Watched by every human love'. Clearly love is being personified. Equally clearly we are not meant to envisage 'loves' fluttering round in the form of guardian angels – something quite out of keeping with the irreligious element in the poem. What seems more likely is that Auden had in mind the guardian *sylphs* of Pope's *Rape of the Lock*, who looked after Belinda's dreams. This would fit in well enough with 'the involuntary powers' which must be those of the unconscious, and with the most plausible interpretation of 'nights of insult' as those of nightmare. Moreover, it would refer the perceptive reader to a charming fiction, appropriately allowing the poet to utter a heartfelt wish while avoiding the traps of sentimentality on the one hand or complicated psychological explanation on the other.

The Capital

Quarter of pleasures where the rich are always waiting,
Waiting expensively for miracles to happen,
O little restaurant where the lovers eat each other,
Café where exiles have established a malicious village;

You with your charm and your apparatus have abolished
The strictness of winter and the spring's compulsion;
Far from your lights the outraged punitive father,
The dullness of mere obedience here is apparent.

Yet with orchestras and glances, O, you betray us
To belief in our infinite powers; and the innocent
Unobservant offender falls in a moment
Victim to the heart's invisible furies.

In unlighted streets you hide away the appalling;
Factories where lives are made for a temporary use
Like collars or chairs, rooms where the lonely are battered
Slowly like pebbles into fortuitous shapes.

But the sky you illumine, your glow is visible far
Into the dark countryside, the enormous, the frozen,
Where, hinting at the forbidden like a wicked uncle,
Night after night to the farmer's children you beckon.   (1938)
                        (*Selected Poems*, p. 78. *Collected Poems*, p. 145)

With hindsight it is difficult not to see in 'The Capital' signs that Auden's atheistic period was ending. Not that it is in any way a religious poem; in so far as it deals with the duality of man and his environment it does so implicitly in terms of Ego and Id, Rural and Urban, rather than in terms of moral choice or the World and the Wholly Other. Similarly, something of the early social concern is evident in the fourth stanza. Nevertheless, there are signs of change. Obedience no longer seems to be disparaged in favour of freedom (especially sexual freedom). If there is a touch of the old irony in 'the outraged punitive father', which clearly refers to the Freudian God as well as the literal parent, so also is there a touch of irony in that 'mere' which qualifies obedience. If it still seems necessary not to repress basic drives into the subconscious where they may turn into 'invisible furies', it is notable that falling a victim to such energies is said to be due, not to repressive conventional morality, but to a misguided belief in human omnipotence ('our infinite powers'). And the poem as a whole, though curious rather than censorious, seems to come down against the temptations of worldly sophistication offered by the capital.

The capital, like all other cities in Auden, is not any city in particular; it is an archetypal capital, a distillation of all the capitals one has known or read of: a myth-city, which can therefore be associated with something in the psyche, and plausibly be personified as the legendary 'wicked uncle'. Nothing about it is being 'proved on the pulses'; the appeal is to the conceptual imagination. Indeed, the real subject seems to be, not 'you' (the city), but 'us' (the human). Appropriately enough, then, the presentation is somewhat symbolic, reminiscent of a play or an expressionist film where lighting is part of meaning.

This characteristic is emphasised a little more in the revised version of the *Collected Poems*, which has 'Dim-lighted restaurant' instead of 'O little restaurant'. But even as it stands, lighting is implicit or explicit in every stanza. A 'Quarter of pleasures', almost by definition, is brightly and variously lit, and makes a stark contrast with the poor quarter of a city, with its 'unlighted streets'. Similarly, the city as a whole, with its 'lights', contrasts with the natural world subject to seasonal light and dark; and the city's warm 'glow', a suspect illumination in the sky – like pie in the sky – acts as a temptation to the 'dark countryside'. The chiaroscuro of this poem, then, is tonally significant. It acts as an extra image, in a work that could easily have become prosy. One other reason that it does not, is that its ideas are converted into a series of vignettes; the verbal camera cuts from one illustrative scene to another, leaving each to explain itself, and all to comment, by contrast, on each other.

That the poem is essentially didactic rather than lyrical is underlined by the form, of loose unrhymed syllabics that encourage no escape from considering implications. But the didacticism is lightened by evocations of Victorian melodrama, and the diction and syntax are clear and precise. That the rich are 'always' waiting, and waiting 'expensively' points to a permanent human proclivity: to imagine that money is a panacea. But there are some things money can't buy, as 'miracles' confirms. The dim lights of the lovers' restaurant are romantic enough, but the romanticism is wittily cancelled by the idea of mutual greedy possessiveness given in 'eat each other'. And the café's presumably rather brighter lighting only shows up the ignoble side of political exiles – and also complicates the contrast of city and country by indicating the prevalence of gossip in villages (a curse that citizens are relatively free of, if only because nobody cares about anybody in a capital city). In like way, 'apparatus', in the second stanza, drastically qualifies the favourable connotations of 'charm', since the line incongruously juxtaposes items from a humane and an experimental register. So whether it is a good or a bad thing to have avoided 'The strictness of winter and the spring's compulsion' becomes ambiguous. Since 'charm' is not so favourable as, say, 'friendliness', however, it tends to be somewhat overruled by 'apparatus', and thus the balance is rather weighed down against the abolition of natural conditioning and (as the last lines of this and the following stanza suggest) inner discipline and spontaneous sexual love. That is why a certain irony seems to attach to '*mere* obedience' and why 'the outraged punitive father' seems, though melodramatic, not to be entirely ridiculous.

The puritanism of the next stanza confirms this sense of a balance weighted *against* the capital, and *for* something harsher and more natural (though less immediately likable). That confirmation is carried mainly by the use of 'betray' for the pleasures or charm of 'orchestras and glances', and is perhaps made slightly more evident by the substitution of 'So' for 'Yet' in the revised version (which also eliminates the rhetorical 'O' in favour of 'soon' – suggestive of rapid corruption). In any case, the next stanza makes clear the illusory nature of the glamour of the big city, by turning to its seamy side: the badly lit districts of those who support the rich waiting expensively in the bright quarter of pleasures. 'Hide away' suggests a guilty secret – and indeed such discrepancies are an indictment of *capital*ism; yet the stanza is in fact much more psychological than political. It is the oddity and suffering of the lonely that is emphasised, rather than the deprivation of the poor. 'Factories' certainly calls to mind the industrial proletariat, but since real factories don't turn out lives *for* use (they make use *of* lives to turn out objects) the word has to be taken metaphorically. It makes sense if taken to refer to the depressed areas, the unlighted streets, where people were turned out only for a life of work – while jobs were available.

The final stanza is entirely in long-shot. From a great distance we see the capital as a diffuse glow in the night sky: temptation made visible. It could be a haven, a heaven, for those whose lot it is to have been cast into the outer darkness, the enormous frozen countryside. By adding these qualities to those of 'strictness', 'compulsion', and 'dullness', life associated with the farm is made to seem far from romantically agreeable. One can see why the farmer's children should be attracted to the capital – or, in psychological terms, why the innocent should be tempted to false quests, quests that will lead to hell, which also glows, rather than heaven – or at least to a place where they will fall victim to the 'furies', receive *capital* punishment instead of, or because of, having a capital good time.

We have been shown 'the *capital*' at close quarters and seen its attractions to be at best superficial. Hence the aptness of 'forbidden' and the reasonableness of detecting in 'wicked uncle' a hint of a comic Satan. '*The* forbidden' – that is, the class of all that is forbidden – tends to support the idea that by the end of the poem *the* capital (by now, whatever seems 'capital'?) has become almost wholly a psychological metaphor for temptation in general. We are almost within sight of the ideal Good Place, the Just City, that Auden was soon to set against the actual, as the visionary goal of an endless but true quest.

6 Poems of the 'American' Period

For all his agreement with Marx about the iniquity of alienation there is a sense in which alienation suited Auden. It suited his tendencies to cranky individualism and to taking a detached overview. So America served him well; by cutting him off from his roots it freed him from parochialism and from the obligation to be a leader of the Left. He could now believe whatever he liked, or try out beliefs to see if he liked them. True, he had adopted a new ideology: that of existentialist Christianity. But that proved in practice to be less imprisoning than it might have been. For one thing, as we have seen, Kierkegaard's doctrine of the fallenness of the world combined with the unknowableness of the divine – a source of anxiety for him – allowed Auden to accept the imperfections of man, nature, and society with wry gladness; and therefore to write, of what had to be endured since it could not be cured, in the mode of mithridatic, or even celebratory comedy. For another thing, after the brief period of convertite enthusiasm, he came to believe that there should not be, and indeed was not, any such thing as Christian art. In 'Christianity and Art' (*Selected Essays*) he argues that it would be wrong to make an aesthetic object for public entertainment out of one's feelings of penitence and guilt before God. So there is only art in a Christian spirit, and a still-life, in that sense, may well be more Christian than a Crucifixion. These two factors allowed his ingrained liberalism to dominate his dogmatic existentialism, at any rate in poetic practice – a process no doubt further encouraged by two new literary beliefs: first, that poetry is primarily a verbal game, and second, that the true poet finds in arbitrary technical difficulties a source of ideas (which means that a poem is not limited to ideas derived from the poet's ostensible beliefs, but is also open to those prompted by, for example, the demands of rhyme).

By this time, he had come to see Marxism itself in terms of Freud, as a theory springing from father-domination: a vast rationalisation in fact; and his only political interest now lay in encouraging a climate of life that would allow the individual's inner self to flourish.

How far this was a *personal* development it is difficult to say. C. Day Lewis, who was a Communist Party member in the Thirties, became an Anglican, Professor of Poetry at Oxford (like Auden), Poet Laureate, and a C.B.E. Stephen Spender, also a Party member, became a C.B.E., a respectable literary editor, and a university professor. So, too, Charles Madge and Rex Warner became university

Auden at a poetry reading after his return to Christ Church, in Oxford, in 1972

professors, and Louis MacNeice, after a stint in university teaching, joined the staff of the B.B.C. This question, however, has no *direct* bearing on the quality of the poetry. One of the prerequisites for a great poet is that his work should do more than merely reflect the spirit of the age. Close analysis has shown this to be true even of Auden's work in his 'committed' period; of his later work it shows it to be even truer.

The Fall of Rome

The piers are pummelled by the waves;
In a lonely field the rain
Lashes an abandoned train;
Outlaws fill the mountain caves.

Fantastic grow the evening gowns;
Agents of the Fisc pursue
Absconding tax-defaulters through
The sewers of provincial towns.

Private rites of magic send
The temple prostitutes to sleep;
All the literati keep
An imaginary friend.

Cerebrotonic Catos may
Extol the Ancient Disciplines,
But the muscle-bound Marines
Mutiny for food and pay.

Caesar's double-bed is warm
As an unimportant clerk
Writes I DO NOT LIKE MY WORK
On a pink official form.

Unendowed with wealth or pity,
Little birds with scarlet legs,
Sitting on their speckled eggs,
Eye each flu-infected city.

Altogether elsewhere, vast
Herds of reindeer move across
Miles and miles of golden moss,
Silently and very fast.   (1947)
(*Selected Poems*, p. 183. *Collected Poems*, p. 257)

The commonest kind of ballad consists of rhymed couplets, each line being composed of seven iambic feet, a form once known as 'fourteeners' on account of the long fourteen-syllable line. Such ballads, however, usually take some liberties with syllabic regularity, whether for purposes of the story, or to accommodate features of the music they were sung to, or simply by way of inheritance from the English poetry preceding the traditional ballad: a poetry based on sprung-rhythm (counting only stressed syllables) rather than metre. Usually the lines of the couplet were split to form quatrains with four and three stresses to each pair of lines. This led, fairly often, to the unrhymed first and third lines being given a rhyme, so that many ballads come to be made up of quatrains stressed 4, 3:4, 3 and rhyming ab:ab. That is to say, they are rather more formal than the original long, loose couplet, and the writer needs to work somewhat harder to maintain the clarity of narrative needed for something to be taken in, along with music, at first hearing.

Auden carries this sophisticating process further. This poem still fulfils what remain prime requirements of a ballad, though it is no longer necessarily written for music: namely, that it should tell a story, and tell it clearly in uncomplicated syntax and normal idiom. In fact, Auden's poem has *no* figures of speech; it relies entirely on the effect of the facts and incidents recounted. All traces of the original couplet form disappear. There is no tendency for the sense-units to end with the second line, nor is there any tendency for one stanza to lead on to the next in a continuous story-line. On the contrary, the novel rhyme-scheme, abba, ensures that each stanza closes in upon itself – and *this* tallies with the sense-units. The poem remains, however, in a quite central sense of the word, a narrative. It tells of the fall of Rome, and the tale is full of action; its incidents are arresting, its verbs active and in the present tense. But the method is that of montage. One 'shot' is juxtaposed with another so that we get a panoramic picture of collapse.

The present tense brings us into that picture – appropriately, for items in the content indicate that *our* civilisation also is involved. Trains and pink paper are latterday properties. Indeed, there are hints that the Roman Empire stands for all the great civilisations that have foundered. The literati's keeping an imaginary friend recalls the Italian Renaissance, the temple prostitutes, the past glories of India (though no doubt they were to be found in parts of the Roman Empire too). The montage method is equally appropriate, since what we are being told of is not the local sequence of personal events characteristic of the traditional ballad but rather of a simultaneous crumbling affecting everyone, a whole great order staggering into chaos. On such a subject, Auden's preference for the panoramic really comes into its own. So too does his command of form, for its precision and varied repetitiveness – all rhymes, including 'clerk', being full rhymes, all stanzas closed stanzas – help to suggest the accuracy of the report and the inevitability of the process reported.

The first suggestion is, of course, particularly necessary as Auden's universalising of the theme takes the subject-matter out of the realm of history into that of myth: the realm of general, not specific, import. Myth of this kind accords with Aristotle's observation that the fictions of Greek drama were truer than history, as history deals only with what actually happens, in all its confusion, whereas the fictions deal with a *type* of happening, shown in all the purity of principle – rather as a scientific law will be better revealed in a laboratory demonstration than amongst the clutter of daily life. So, if Auden starts from Gibbon's *Decline and Fall of the Roman Empire*, as he clearly does, he neither uses its actual details (but rather invented details typical of it) nor, as we have seen, does he remain limited to it. As Venus is the type of erotic love, anywhere anytime, so Rome's is taken as the type of any such decline and fall; thus this poem, like all myths, can apply as much to the present or future as to the past.

Even when Auden uses the myth-method in a psychological poem, to dramatise inner forces of the human psyche, there is normally no personal reference. As one would expect, such impersonal penetration to the heart of the matter is even more obviously characteristic of poems dealing in social forces. In 'The Fall of Rome', despite the involving effect of the active verbs and present tense, readers, like the writer, are not emotionally engulfed by the doom portrayed (and prophesied). Instead, they share a god's-eye view, wryly perceiving the presence of the Absurd in both the general picture and the detail. The panoramic sweep clearly contributes to this detachment; and so does the insistent form; but it is the presence of the Antipoet, entertaining us with details of collapse that are curious and unexpected rather than cataclysmic or horrific, that mainly gives the portrait a mask more comic than tragic. The large-scale structure of the poem, however, also contributes something to that mode, for the first five stanzas, detailing the fall, are put into an ironic perspective by the last two which counterpoint the civilised world, in absurd chaos, by a vision of the self-regulating world of nature, 'unendowed' but dignified in its aloofness, and more likely to last.

Looked at a little more closely that structure is seen to consist of five vignettes covering the world of man – in rural, urban, cultural, political, and bureaucratic stanzas, respectively – and two covering the non-human denizens of the earth – those of the air, and those of the land. In short, there is a wide spread, not of figurative rhetoric, but of examples.

The only textural devices of rhetoric, apart from those of rhyme and metre already discussed, are certain variations of rhythm and instances of alliteration that are purposeful in effect – though they occur so naturally that they seem the result of chance (or perhaps one should say the result of the poet's happening to be 'on form' during this particular verbal game).

The plosive alliteration of 'piers' and 'pummelling' certainly reinforces the sense of the opening line – an arresting symbolic shot anyway. Rhythmically, 'Lashes' gains extra force by breaking the iambic base-pattern, so that two stressed syllables come together to emphasise the misery: 'ráin/Láshes'. The last line of the stanza cuts to another aspect of the unhappy rural scene (so different from the pastoral paradises of literary antiquity), but there is presumably a connection between the emptiness of the field and the presence of nearby outlaws, as well as a connection with the violent rain – a concatenation hinted at, anyway, by the labial alliteration of the last three lines of the stanza.

In the following 'urban' stanza, 'Fisc' and 'defaulters' are linked by sense as well as sound. Nor is the initial letter of 'Fantastic' as irrelevant as it might seem. Rhyme links the first and last lines, which appear to be opposite in sense, but the final picture is one of decadence on the surface and decadence below it – in each case a decadence of extravagance. So, 'Fantastic' ties in with 'Fisc' and '-fault'.

Culture in the wider sense – in which the word is related both to 'cult' and 'cultivation' – seems to be the underlying concern of the third stanza. The first sense-unit deals with religion, the second with literature, and both are seen as decadent – a linking encouraged by the rhyme-scheme which crosses the sense-boundary. Both present a sexual decadence. Public veneration of sex and fertility, signified by the temple prostitutes, has declined into 'Private rites of magic', the prostitutes no longer being called upon; and the literary people write not of real, but imaginary mistresses. The impotence already seen in the area of administrative order seems to be reflected in culture's retreat from the real.

Passing to the political, Auden uses contrast rather than comparison, the mind/body theme for once being mediated in social terms. Again the realm of brain is related to that of brawn formally as well as semantically, through the tactful alliteration of '-brotonic' and '-bound' and of 'may', 'muscle', 'Marines' and 'Mutiny'. 'Ancient Disciplines' ironically reminds the reader that for what we call 'ancient' Rome this was a modern period. A reminder that moves us on to a stanza strongly suggestive of our own time. The clerk with the American accent, so to speak, is a crucial sign that Caesar's sense of security is illusory. Civilisation, alas, depends on bureaucracy. So it is not accidental, but of the essence of the grimly comic structure that this, the most trifling of the signs of breakdown, is the clinching one.

With the doom of civilisation inevitable, the god's-eye turns suddenly to that world of existential otherness, of creatures that are never absurd and always blameless. In each of these concluding stanzas the sense runs through without a break; this is not a realm of disintegration. That it is a poorer realm, and pitiless, lends an extra sadness to the failure of man's great endeavour (this is mithridatic, not satirical – and certainly not celebratory – comedy).

The birds are sitting pretty, in every sense of the phrase, their natural health and beauty contrasting with the sickness of the decaying city (a relationship again underlined by the alliteration of 'sitting' etc. with 'city'). Finally, 'Altogether elsewhere' – in place, in time-scale, in social order – the reindeer move like ghosts, 'Silently and very fast' through a great world of alien beauty ('across/Miles and miles of golden moss'). An otherness subtly emphasised by a network of now differently operating alliteration: of s's, v's, and m's, mild and gentle sounds knitting together a world separate from, and wordlessly reproving, that of 'Rome'.

So a brilliant change of perspective ends a brilliant poem on perspectives of change.

Song – *Deftly, admiral, cast your fly*

Deftly, admiral, cast your fly
　　Into the slow deep hover,
Till the wise old trout mistake and die;
　　Salt are the deeps that cover
　　The glittering fleets you led,
　　　　White is your head.

Read on, ambassador, engrossed
　　In your favourite Stendhal;
The Outer Provinces are lost,
　　Unshaven horsemen swill
　　The great wines of the Chateaux
　　　　Where you danced long ago.

Do not turn, do not lift, your eyes
　　Toward the still pair standing
On the bridge between your properties,
　　Indifferent to your minding:
　　In its glory, in its power,
　　　　This is their hour.

Nothing your strength, your skill, could do
　　Can alter their embrace
Or dispersuade the Furies who
　　At the appointed place
　　With claw and dreadful brow
　　　　Wait for them now.　　　　(1948)
(*Selected Poems*, p. 187. *Collected Poems*, p. 437)

Once more, a poem dealing with the disasters of Time, but in this case – though it is an even shorter poem than 'The Fall of Rome' – including the personal and psychological as well as the social and political. In marvellously deft verse, deep themes are brought to a glittering surface. Perfectly ordinary diction, idiom, and syntax are wrought into a whole as profound and magical in its effect as a classic fairy-tale. It is sad and light, distancing and detailed, simple yet far from simplistic; theme and treatment modulate in beautiful balance like shot silk. This must surely rank among the great lyrics of the language.

If, that is, we call it a lyric. In so far as it is put forward as a song, is short clear and moving as a song should be, and could perfectly well be set to music, it would come under the traditional heading of 'lyric'. In so far as the writer's relationship with his audience is not direct and subjective (nor quite indirect as in drama)but mediate, it would count as 'narrative'. Moreover, it does tell a short story, complete with a twist in the tail. The poem, that is to say, is delicately poised between lyric form and narrative content, deriving tonal benefit from the one, and thematic scope from the other.

Structurally, the poem presents a symbolic tableau, the admiral and the ambassador on their respective territories, appropriately still concerned with water and words, with the lovers on the bridge between: Force and Finesse (variants of Matter and Mind) with Love bridging the gap; and all three seen as failing. The empire, like the lovers, has its hour ('The glittering fleets', 'the great wines of the Chateaux'); the lovers, like the empire, cannot hold off forever the barbarian 'Furies'.

On a smaller scale too, in the structure and texture of the separate stanzas the personal and the political are parallelled – with great subtlety and profundity despite the surface simplicity of style. Since the admiral outwits the wise old trout, he is clearly no fool; his deftness, therefore, from the start carries overtones of cleverness. Nevertheless he lost his fleets. He himself was perhaps a wise old trout outwitted by some subtler angler – Time? Weather? A greater admiral? We do not know. Perhaps he does not. It is difficult not to see at least a hint of psychological symbolism in the first two lines: the conscious intelligence casting about for answers in the unknown – the neologism 'hover' implying uncertainty – trying to bring up representatives of the glittering fleets below the surface. Various reverberations elsewhere in the stanza tend to support this hint. 'Deep' is echoed in the fourth line. Now, plainly the primary sense is simply that of an ironic comment, reinforced by the metrical stress on 'Salt': 'freshwater covers the glittering trout, saltwater your fleets – so how deft and clever are you?' But 'Salt' surely suggests bitter? Indeed, '*Bitter* the deeps . . .' would have made an ironically appropriate rhyme with 'glitter-'. Possibly too obviously appropriate. But 'salt' has another advantage: it matches 'White' in the last line. His head is covered by the salt of time – which not only implies the bitterness of age and links up with bitterness about the lost fleets, but also supports the hint of symbolism mentioned: that the 'deep hover' and the salt 'deeps' represent at a secondary level depths inside the head. Does this still seem far-fetched? It should not; 'Soul and body have no bounds' for Auden; and it would be quite in keeping with his fondness for progressive change (rather than simple repetition) for him to have the poem turn slowly inside out, as it seems to: the destructive Furies of the lovers clearly being primarily psychological ones (waiting '*now*') and only secondarily those of physical old age. It is worth noting in passing the varied precision of the diction: the three stressed vowels of 'slow deep hover', the literal element in 'mis-take' (a bait), or the touch of Bunteresque slang in 'wise old trout' that permits a human association.

Turning from the military to the diplomatic, we find the ambassador, like the admiral, brought into the tableau as an almost tangible presence by the mode of direct address. But whereas the admiral was, literally, engaged in a physical activity the ambassador is engaged in a mental one – appositely reading Stendhal, that civilised, cynical connoisseur of curious conscience. This tallies with Auden's view that the adage 'If you can't beat 'em, join 'em' is wrong, that on the contrary it is admirable to fiddle while Rome burns, to keep high culture going to the last. The latter part of the stanza uses history, as in 'The Fall of Rome', in a mythical way. It is typical of all great empires that the Outer Provinces fall first to the barbarians, that riot and loot hold them up for a time, perhaps a very long time, owing to the corrupting of vigour by easy living, so that life at the centre can go on unchanged, if under threat. The ruin of civilised values is swiftly conveyed by 'Unshaven', 'swill', and 'danced', but 'long ago' indicates that the ambassador is of the same generation as the admiral. Presumably diplomacy and the army, like the fleet, have failed to hold off the invaders. In the light of what we know of the ambassador's age, however, and of the overtones in the first stanza, one almost inescapably also takes the Outer Provinces to symbolise the body, under attack by the same enemy that bleached the hair and embittered the mind of the admiral.

'Glory' and 'power' in the next stanza, since they are normally used in public contexts, particularly those of war, clearly relate personal to national history, the inevitable defeat of the individual to that of the state – and this strongly validates the duplex interpretation of the first two stanzas.

'Do not turn' must refer to the fishing admiral; 'do not lift' to the reading ambassador, which makes it evident that the 'strength' and 'skill' of the final stanza refer, respectively, to them too. Thus both are kept in mind to the end, and are shown to represent major powers of both the person and the state. By analogy, then, as well as by their position ('on the bridge') the lovers come to represent not only a personal force more powerful and glorious than the forces of strength and skill, but also that social binding force without which all the efforts of military and diplomatic corps will be unavailing.

Had the poem ended at this point it might have been justly stigmatised as sentimental, or at least limited, but this is precisely the point – four lines from the end – at which we get the twist in the tail, when what has been latent throughout suddenly is made manifest: that the ultimate enemies, inevitably defeating everyone, body and soul, are Time, Age, and Human Nature.

Whether the final sense of serene wisdom distilled into words is due to Auden's later religious conviction as to the ultimate worth of any kind of worldly power or glory is a matter of opinion. It may simply be due to his perceptiveness and honesty. Whatever the extra-literary cause there certainly is this effect, of wise truth. But the uncanny sense of cogency in its delivery is a triumph of technique – without which no one would take notice of the wisest truth. So this poem, like many another of Auden's, though it may not prove its point 'on the pulses' in a Keatsian way, does *prove* it, as every poem should, by means significantly different from those of rational prose.

Bucolics: Woods

Sylvan meant savage in those primal woods
Piero di Cosimo so loved to draw,
Where nudes, bears, lions, sows with women's heads
Mounted and murdered and ate each other raw,
Nor thought the lightening-kindled bush to tame
But flabbergasted, fled the useful flame.

Reduced to patches owned by hunting squires
Of villages with ovens and [a] stocks, [*corrected from C.P.*]
They whispered still of most unsocial fires,
Though Crown and Mitre warned their silly flocks
The pasture's humdrum rhythms to approve
And to abhor the license of the grove.

Guilty intention still looks for a hotel
That wants no details and surrenders none;
A wood is that, and throws in charm as well,
And many a semi-innocent, undone,
Has blamed its nightingales who round the deed
Sang with such sweetness of a happy greed.

Those birds, of course, did nothing of the sort,
And, as for sylvan nature, if you take
A snapshot at a picnic, O how short
And lower-ordersy the Gang will look
By those vast lives that never took another
And are not scared of gods, ghosts, or stepmother.

Among these coffins of its by-and-by
The Public can (it cannot on a coast)
Bridle its skirt-and-bargain chasing eye,
And where should an austere philologist
Relax but in the very world of shade
From which the matter of his field was made.

Old sounds re-educate an ear grown coarse,
As Pan's green father suddenly raps out
A burst of undecipherable Morse,
And cuckoos mock in Welsh, and doves create

In rustic English all they do
To rear their modern family of two.

Now here, now there, some loosened element,
A fruit in vigour or a dying leaf,
Utters its private idiom for descent,
And late man, listening through his latter grief,
Hears, close or far, the oldest of his joys,
Exactly as it was, the water noise.

A well-kempt forest begs Our Lady's grace;
Someone is not disgusted, or at least
Is laying bets upon the human race
Retaining enough decency to last;
The trees encountered on a country stroll
Reveal a lot about that country's soul.

A small grove massacred to the last ash,
An oak with heart-rot, give away the show:
This great society is going smash;
They cannot fool us with how fast they go,
How much they cost each other and the gods!
    A culture is no better than its woods.   (1952)
        (*Selected Poems*, p. 204. *Collected Poems*, p. 427)

Auden's geography, it has been said, is always psychological. In so
far as nature poetry counts as geographical the statement is less than
the whole truth. What *is* true, is that Auden never sees nature in any of
the traditional ways. He does not portray it, like the Georgians, as
scenery, or like nineteenth-century poets hold it up as an example to
(or escape from) the industrial city, or, like the Romantics, take it as a
material expression of the Absolute or Spirit of the Universe or the
inner spirit of man; nor does he regard it, like many seventeenth- and
eighteenth-century poets as a way to God through His creation.
Auden's nature poetry is unique in the amazing variety of other ways
in which it works. It is not only psychological, but sociological,
philosophical, ecological, historical, economic, cultural . . . .

How does this square with Auden's existentialist belief in the
'otherness' of nature – a belief, of course, that is itself consistent with
the Christianity he had come to profess, which also regards man not
simply as a natural higher animal but a unique ensouled being? At first
sight it does not square very well – and indeed it should be said that
Auden's nature poems are primarily poems about man. Perhaps 'In
Praise of Limestone' shows that most clearly. The various landscapes it
deals with are not revealed in local particularity; they are examples of
that *type* of landscape, and are mainly of interest for the light they
throw on types of man: those found appropriate to one kind of habitat
or another. So also with the *Bucolics*; mountains, plains, and streams

are seen as attracting different kinds of people or as being relatable to different aspects of *human* nature. However, it could be argued that by relating natural scenes to human concerns the poems do gradually reveal the essential character of those scenes themselves. To the extent that this is true it can be said that Auden's nature poetry does square with his philosophical view of nature. It is not, however, true to any great extent, for though, say, mountains, plains and streams differ, they do not really have any *character* (they are just neutral matter differently arranged). So in defining their 'essence' by that particular spectrum of ways in which they can aptly be related to man, the poet is again really talking of man, but less directly. And this, it is arguable, is not only a unique kind of nature poetry; it is the only really sensible kind.

'Woods' has all the special qualities of Auden's later nature poetry. A comic affection for the foibles of fallen man, and for the characteristics of the woods of his environment, is rendered in an endlessly varied sequence of fascinating reflections, all delivered in the style of an urbane lively conversationalist, whose intelligent entertaining talk happens to fall into an agreeable form. That form is a loosely metred iambic pentameter, regularly but loosely rhymed; the tone sardonic, parodic, self-mocking in turn but underlain throughout by a humorous seriousness. The first two stanzas sketch the relationship of woods to prehistorical and historical man, the next five to contemporary man, and the last two conclude by reflecting on the significance of the relationships. Those dealt with may be roughly classified, in order, as psychological, religious, amorous, moral, practical, cultural, and social.

Such a rough sketch, however, does little justice to the poem's special qualities, in particular to its modulations of feeling, from joky intellectualism through affectionate mockery to a sadly guarded optimism; nor does it do justice to the elegant blend of wit, learning, perceptiveness, and bright ideas.

The first stanza recalls the days when primitive man barely held his own, as hunter, against the creatures hunting him; when the primal woods, especially at night, were presumably places of fear. One says 'presumably' because such days are prehistorical, so that the feelings of our remote forebears must be deduced from legend, myth, surviving jungle tribes – uncertainly known from anthropological research – and the evidence of probability (after all, it *ought* to have been nightmarish to live in danger of being murdered or eaten; so one's inclined to give credence to the psychological theory that certain fears are a primal inheritance). The stanza, however, makes no attempt to recreate such nightmare feelings. It recalls them, with civilised curiosity, through the perspective of Renaissance Italy and the quizzing-glass of Augustan England: two of the most sophisticated periods in history. Piero di Cosimo, a contemporary of Leonardo, was no primitive, nor did Renaissance Italy have any direct experience of primal woods; and 'loved to draw' suggests the primitivism of blasé sophistication – and it is at *that*, surely, that the mild fun is directed ('Mounted and murdered and ate each other raw' – without so much as pausing for a comma). A similar, but not identical tone, pervades the last two lines, which parody many complacent eighteenth-century comments on the short-comings of less rational peoples.

The next stanza takes us into historical times, more medieval than anything else (though the opening lines suggest a rather later period); a time when Christianity had still not quite taken, and people retained folk-customs that were relics of ancient fertility religion. 'Silly' in the fourth line seems to be used, aptly enough, in its earlier sense of 'simple'. 'Abhor', too, carries just a touch of the period vocabulary of official warning.

The third stanza brings us to the present, when woods are not dangerous but inviting, especially to lovers. The diction now incorporates a modern slangy idiom that contributes to an increasingly bantering tone ('throws in charm', 'A semi-innocent') – both characteristics being sustained through the next stanza, which begins the section of reflective commentary. That stanza debunks the pastoral's idea of the greater dignity of man in a rural setting, by a nice play on 'short' and 'lower'. The comparison with trees is both physical and moral – though not entirely serious, as the collocation of 'gods, ghosts, or stepmother' indicates.

The fifth stanza turns to more material relationships: trees provide coffins and books for mankind; they are a matter of life and death for us. Something of the austere dignity of woods, as well as philologists, comes through, and thus makes a transition to the paradoxical cultural stanza – the need for the book-learned to re-learn the language of nature (wittily conveyed as the forest's 'undecipherable Morse'). It is not quite clear whether the next line is mocking the reader, the Welsh, or the cuckoo; but if one calls to mind the Welsh inflexion of 'Look you', it may simply seem a bit of humorous philology. The doves more obviously match motherly fussing and cooing over infants.

More seriously, and indeed beautifully, the next stanza pursues the topic of the language of nature. The wit is profound rather than flippant. In the vigour of youth or in old age some natural force may cut us from our life-support; in any case we are always heading for a fall. Nature's messages are not easy to decipher, since the language of different elements is neither common nor public. Such seem to be the implications of the first three lines, the fourth line making a bridge from this sad truth to its compensation. 'Late man': appearing after the other creatures, and therefore late in learning the language and the truths of nature. He has to listen hard 'through his latter grief' – the grief, we may assume from other poems, of an evolved consciousness able to feel guilt and dread – but also to aspire and appreciate. Auden's 'Song for St Cecilia's Day' and the conclusion of 'In Praise of

Auden's apartment at 77 St Mark's Place, New York, in 1972

Limestone' are both relevant to the implications of the last lines of the stanza.

The final stanzas of this poem, summing up the social significance of woods, need little comment. Auden's gift for seeing large significances in small details has been noted earlier, as has his growing interest in ecology, and the talent for aphorism (particularly evident at the end of each stanza here) that gives a tighter conclusion to a generally affable easy-mannered poem.

The farmhouse at Kirchstetten, near Vienna, which inspired About the House *from which is taken 'The Geography of the House'*

Thanksgiving for a Habitat: The Geography of the House

Seated after breakfast
In this white-tiled cabin
Arabs call *the House where
Everybody goes*,
Even melancholics
Raise a cheer to Mrs
Nature for the primal
Pleasures She bestows.

Sex is but a dream to
Seventy-and-over,
But a joy proposed un-
-til we start to shave:
Mouth-delight depends on
Virtue in the cook, but
This She guarantees from
Cradle unto grave.

Lifted off the potty,
Infants from their mothers
Hear their first impartial
Words of worldly praise:
Hence, to start the morning
With a satisfactory
Dump is a good omen
All our adult days.

Revelation came to
Luther in a privy
(Crosswords have been solved there):
Rodin was no fool
When he cast his Thinker,
Cogitating deeply,
Crouched in the position
Of a man at stool.

All the Arts derive from
This ur-act of making,
Private to the artist:
Makers' lives are spent
Striving in their chosen
Medium to produce a
De-narcissus-ized en-
-during excrement.

Freud did not invent the
Constipated miser:

Banks have letter boxes
Built in their facade,
Marked *For Night Deposits*,
Stocks are firm or liquid,
Currencies of nations
Either soft or hard.

Global Mother, keep our
Bowels of compassion
Open through our lifetime,
Purge our minds as well:
Grant us a kind ending,
Not a second childhood,
Petulant, weak-sphinctered,
In a cheap hotel.

Keep us in our station:
When we get pound-noteish,
When we seem about to
Take up Higher Thought,
Send us some deflating
Image like the painted ex-
-pression on a Major
Prophet taken short.

(Orthodoxy ought to
Bless our modern plumbing:
Swift and St. Augustine
Lived in centuries
When a stench of sewage
Ever in the nostrils
Made a strong debating
Point for Manichees.)

Mind and Body run on
Different timetables:
Not until our morning
Visit here can we
Leave the dead concerns of
Yesterday behind us,
Face with all our courage
What is now to be.   (1964)
                  (*Selected Poems*, p. 261. *Collected Poems*, p. 526)

The absurd euphemism of the title would alone be sufficient to
indicate, were indication needed, that this is a light-verse poem.
Persona and readers are tuned to the same wavelength from the
beginning, while tone and diction alike are chatty. This is far from

anything we could call nature poetry, though 'Nature' forms its structural backbone. However, temporarily accepting the extended use of 'geography', we can say that this poem too shows Auden's geography to be far more than psychological, for the physiological 'Nature' of the bowels – an inherently unpromising subject one might think – is here related knowingly to man in more than a score of ways. Again, a fountaining forth of bright ideas: clever, amusing, wise, even (on reflection) moving, in turn – and, like a fountain, the form maintains a pleasing unity-in-variety.

The first six stanzas may be considered as 'the cheer' for Nature referred to in the sixth line, the next three stanzas constituting a prayer to Nature, and the final stanza a natural conclusion to the whole. To put it another way: the first six stanzas deal with loo-related concerns of the past and present, the next three to those of the future, while the last is a timeless summing-up. The large-scale structure, then, is rational; it is also a bit irregular, for not everything – especially not the parenthetical penultimate stanza – quite fits these broad categories. The further down the scale we go the greater the irregularity, and therefore the more conscious we become, formally, of the variety within the unity.

Every stanza has eight lines, and every fourth line rhymes. We are dealing, that is to say, with enormously long-lined couplets whose rhymes are further separated, both aurally and psychologically, by the triple break in each half. Every short line contains six syllables, save for the rhyming lines which contain five. All this is highly regular and unifying; and it might account for the fact that the rhymes rather surprisingly do chime to the ear, despite the unnatural rhythm imposed by the syllabics. Deliberately unnatural, we may assume, since elsewhere Auden writes syllabics that conform quite effortlessly to the rhythms of sense and natural speech. Here they are usually in counterpoint to them. This means that Auden is choosing to rely far less than most writers of light verse on the snappy aid of rhyme and the lilt of metre – though, again, the poem is nearly metrical, each long line (half-stanza) having between nine and eleven stresses. All in all, however, one is aware of a certain formality shaping the apparently random conversational communication, and aware of its teasing contribution to a generally joky tone; but the attention is not drawn away from the sense to any significant degree.

Every stanza consists of one sentence, divided by a colon (except the first introductory stanza). This does not mean that each stanza expresses just two ideas, but rather that each expresses at least two. Nor does it mean that the sense-breaks in any way correspond with the rhyme-breaks (here too there is counterpointing). Indeed they do not always correspond with the colon-breaks, and the colons occur at very different places in the stanzas, only occasionally coinciding with the rhymes. If we take the poem stanza by stanza, starting in each case at the beginning, then the sense-blocks (which correspond to the number of separate ideas) go as follows: 8 lines/4, 2, 2/4, 4/2, 1, 5/3, 5/2, 3, 1, 2/3, 1, 4/1, 7/2, 6/2, 4, 2. Ten stanzas, regular in number and length of lines, and in rhyme-scheme, irregular in sense-division (no two stanzas being divided alike), and deriving twenty-five distinct ideas, unevenly distributed, from one unpromising subject. In both formal and contentual terms, a remarkable fusion of unity and variety, giving aesthetic pleasure in its own right.

This is not to deny that the chief pleasure of the poem comes from the repeated disclosure of ideas that are amusing but not ridiculous. Yes, how odd – and perversely apt – that revelation should come in a privy! In the light of Freud's remarks on the anal-retentive type, it seems almost credible that the bank and stock-market vocabulary Auden has so brilliantly leapt to must indeed be significant of something in the nature of capitalism and capitalists. And so on.

The prayer section is equally witty in a different way, a more serious way – and interestingly seems to give body precedence over mind, even in fact over religious conviction (while still showing the two as inseparable in such lines as 'Bowels of compassion' and 'Purge our minds as well'). The final stanza picks up this idea, in a conclusion that is not only an end but an inference. Mind and body are still seen as being 'without bounds', but also as being non-coincident. The body runs to chronological time, which is dead as soon as gone; the mind to memory-time, which lingers indefinitely.

A poem, then, formally clever and teasing, cutting across the grain of sense more often than not, contentually stimulating and inventive. But do we, should we, wish for more of what we are used to in poetry: figures of speech or symbolic examples, or more briefly, metaphor and metonymy? There is practically nothing of either – so would it have made an equally good comic essay in prose? Well, obviously no, for the formal reasons already given. But there are other virtues of style worth mentioning: in particular a sense of economy combined with ease that would not have been acceptable in prose. It is the stanza form that allows so many ideas to be offered for inspection in so brief a space. We permit stanzas to be separate brief entities where we should demand greater fullness within, and more explicit connection between prose paragraphs. That we seem not to pay any price for this brevity is not only due to the artificial coherence of a unifying form; it is also due to the fact that the 'lateral' thinking which gives us such a spray of variegated notions is matched by a comparable skill with words, quite different from that of imagery, and in this case more apt. Everything is linked together not by logical, but by psychological connections. Thus, 'the primal pleasures' ending stanza one, makes the imaginative leap to 'sex' seem natural; and sex is not unconnected psychologically with 'mouth-delight' – though the sense actually goes on to cooking. 'Cradle' takes us to 'Infants' and 'grave' to 'All our adult days'.

'Dump' and 'omen' make plausible the leap to Luther's revelation, and 'crosswords' to the 'Thinker': 'Rodin' to the 'Arts' of the next stanza, and the 'ur-act' to 'Freud' in stanza six. 'Nations' at the end of that stanza insensibly makes a bridge from the 'Cheer' to the 'Prayer' section, which begins with 'Global'. 'Keep' in the same line is picked up in the next stanza. 'Cheap' too leads to 'in our station' and 'pound-noteish', 'Higher Thought' to 'Major Prophet', 'Prophet' to 'Orthodoxy', and finally the dualism of Manicheeism to the very different dualism of the timetables of mind and body.

This is light verse, buoyant with its own lack of gravity. There is nothing beyond what we can plainly see, if we look carefully; all the cards are on the table – but very skilfully played. Here, in short, is Uncle Wiz at his most benevolently avuncular, entertaining the company with a new poetry-game.

*The Shield of Achilles**

> She looked over his shoulder
> For vines and olive trees,
> Marble well-governed cities,
> And ships upon untamed seas.
> But there on the shining metal
> His hands had put instead
> An artificial wilderness
> And a sky like lead.

A plain without a feature, bare and brown,
No blade of grass, no sign of neighbourhood,
Nothing to eat and nowhere to sit down,
Yet, congregated on its blankness, stood
An unintelligible multitude,
A million eyes, a million boots in line,
Without expression, waiting for a sign.

Out of the air a voice without a face
Proved by statistics that some cause was just
In tones as dry and level as the place:
No one was cheered and nothing was discussed;
Column by column in a cloud of dust
They marched away enduring a belief
Whose logic brought them, somewhere else, to grief.

> She looked over his shoulder
> For ritual pieties,
> White flower-garlanded heifers,

* Homer's description of the shield of Achilles (*Iliad*, Book XVIII) provides fascinating points of contact with Auden's, and significant differences from it.

Libation and sacrifice,
But there on the shining metal
    Where the altar should have been,
She saw by his flickering forge-light
    Quite another scene.

Barbed wire enclosed an arbitrary spot
    Where bored officials lounged (one cracked a joke)
And sentries sweated, for the day was hot:
    A crowd of ordinary decent folk
    Watched from without and neither moved nor spoke
As three pale figures were led forth and bound
To three posts driven upright in the ground.

The mass and majesty of this world, all
    That carries weight and always weighs the same,
Lay in the hands of others; they were small
    And could not hope for help and no help came:
    What their foes liked to do was done, their shame
Was all the worst could wish; they lost their pride
And died as men before their bodies died.

She looked over his shoulder
    For athletes at their games,
Men and women in a dance
    Moving their sweet limbs
Quick, quick, to music,
    But there on the shining shield
His hands had set no dancing-floor
    But a weed-choked field.

A ragged urchin, aimless and alone,
    Loitered about that vacancy; a bird
Flew up to safety from his well-aimed stone:
    That girls are raped, that two boys knife a third,
    Were axioms to him who'd never heard
Of any world where promises were kept
Or one could weep because another wept.

The thin-lipped armorer,
    Hephaestos, hobbled away;
Thetis of the shining breasts
    Cried out in dismay
At what the god had wrought
    To please her son, the strong
Iron-hearted man-slaying Achilles
    Who would not live long.   (1952)
(*Selected Poems*, p. 198. *Collected Poems*, p. 454)

148

Amidst so much, and such varied work it is difficult, and perhaps invidious, to claim pre-eminence for any one poem. Yet there are grounds for saying that 'The Shield of Achilles' is Auden's greatest poem – at any rate if we agree that the idea of greatness includes a certain degree of public importance and public appeal in a work. It is not easy, indeed, in those terms, to think of a greater poem in this century. One element in its merit is that it combines profound import with utter simplicity. Like most major poets of the modern and post-modern periods, Auden is often obscure, though in the end it is usually possible to understand his work. In this case, however, it is impossible to misunderstand it. The diction is central, the syntax normal and logically ordered, the form heightens without hindering the sense, and the rare rhetorical devices are kept strictly relevant to the needs of theme.

Though not vocative in the way of most odes, but rather a crisp narrative of vivid scenes and actions ('She looked ...', not 'O look ...'), this poem possesses the main features usually associated with the ode: namely, a certain elevation, a sense that the poet is rising above personal matters to speak in a measured responsible way on something of general importance, and the use of a contrasting and comparative method.

What we have throughout is not so much a counterpointing of past and present, or the legendary and the actual, as a timeless contrast and comparison between the arcadian and the utopian (as Auden uses these terms). The arcadian represents the principle of harmony, the utopian that of order; the one community is largely rural and even the people in its small cities have some rapport with nature; the other community is urban-based, complex, overpopulated, and subject to a necessarily highly-organised imposed order. The timeless quality derives in part from the mingled suggestions of the recorded Greek past (in the short-lined stanzas) and the real present (in the others). But more particularly it derives from the use of myth. Hephaestos and Achilles are eternal *types* of the armament manufacturer and the warmonger, the nymph Thetis of the decent humane civilian. As those types are reflected, by implication, in the authoritarians and victims of the 'realistic' stanzas they too are absorbed into the mythic ambiance; so the poem becomes 'not for an age but for all time'.

We said earlier that myth, as used by Auden, is really symbolic metaphor writ large, in that it both concretises and universalises. We might add that it is unlike history because it is not factual, but like history in that it is explanatory; and it is unlike the novel because it is not mimetic, but like the novel in that it is invented. All these features are to be found here. Auden is enabled to present, in its essence, one of the direct forms of 'the baffle of being': the contrast between ideals of harmony and humane community, and practices of mass-manipulation, moral blindness, and militarism; he is able to condense recognisable worlds, as it were, into a timeless metaphor of themselves. To carry our own metaphor further, we could say that the vehicle of the metaphor, that the poem as a whole can be seen as, is the shield, while its tenor is the horrible gap between Ought and Is.

To generalise, we may say that the first three stanzas express the State as organisation, the next three the State as Idea (sublimated into religion and, therefore, involving the persecution of heretics), while the last three exemplify the consequences entailed by such a State. More particularly, the detailed revelation remarkably combines plainness with power, largely because of very subtle stylistic effects and a very cogent choice of metonymic examples.

In this mythicised documentary, as we may style it, the legendary shield is not presented mimetically. Not even a shield fashioned by a god could picture so much – and in any case the scene seems to change every time Thetis looks at it. A magic mirror, revealing the future as well as the present and showing what is true rather than what is desired, is what it really acts as. A device that permits the poet to concentrate great scope in a small compass.

The Grecian stanzas contrast internally as well as contrasting with the (largely) contemporary stanzas. The repetition of the first and fifth lines evokes a sense of humanity's repeated disappointment, as what is hoped for and expected turns into something quite contrary. The last stanza, however, changes the pattern to give a double twist in the tail. The shining metal of the shield, symbol of armaments and death, is replaced by 'the shining breasts' of Thetis, a symbol of beauty and life. We find out, too, that the anonymous 'She' is in fact the mother of Achilles – a reminder of the special griefs of war among the general ones. And the legendary hero (burlesqued by the urchin) is ironically deglamourised as the favourable adjective 'strong' is followed by 'Iron-hearted, man-slaying' and it is revealed that his defensive armament only ensures that he 'would not live long'.

The turn in the first stanza is, of course, intelligent and logical. It would have been hypocritical for an armaments' manufacturer – especially one with a god's vision – to portray scenes worthy of Keats's 'Grecian Urn' on his work. 'An artificial wilderness' is more to the point: 'artificial' because the shield is a work of artifice, and also because war will make a wilderness of what nature and pastoral work have made fruitful (a new twist to Auden's art/nature theme).

A similarly judicious choice of words is found elsewhere: 'congregated', from its association with religious gatherings, takes on a bitter irony, 'unintelligible' suggests not only the mind-boggling vastness of the army, but its meaninglessness (what *sense* can be made of getting half a million men together and turning them into robots?). So too, 'enduring' seems to imply a belief foisted on to people from without, and in context it also hints that it will bring suffering rather than happiness. 'Pale figures' carries overtones of long incarceration as

150

WYSTAN
HUGH
AUDEN
1907–1973

In the prison of his days
Teach the free man
how to praise

Buried
irchstett
wer Aus

Auden's memorial at Poets' Corner, Westminster Abbey

well as fear, and 'vacancy', in the paradoxical context of 'aimless' and 'well-aimed', clearly refers to a moral void as well as a physical wasteland.

The two types of stanza are linked in so far as the longer-lined stanzas tease out in a more documentary way what was implicit in the concise symbolic picture of the shorter-lined stanzas. Stanza-form supports content, though, in a more general sense: such a wide-ranging poem needs not merely the plethora of concrete examples, which give it a body and impact that plain preaching could never achieve, but needs also a corset of regular rhyme and metre to keep them in shape and help them towards an odal dignity. It is one way of attaining elevation without becoming stilted. Where Auden does use language of 'mass and majesty' he is careful to avoid the trap many writers of odes fall into: that of choosing it from a register of special poetic diction. 'An unintelligible multitude', 'An artificial wilderness', 'Libation and sacrifice', 'The mass and majesty of this world', are all made up from everyman's vocabulary. Alliteration, again, is used with extraordinary tact, quite unobtrusively underlining an already powerfully ordered sense. Witness, for instance, the repeated labials of 'An unintelligible multitude/A million eyes, a million boots in line' (one might note also the apt rows of short vowels); or 'could not hope for help and no help came' (noting also the abstention from conventional heroics or lucky escape); or, again, the way these lines are quietly woven together by sound as well as sense: 'any world where promises are kept/Or one could weep because another wept' (noting here, as elsewhere, the sense of measured comment given by parallelism: 'one/another', 'weep/wept').

The panoramic sweep, the slight distancing of the strict form, the measured restraint of the diction, the mythical ambiance, and the prevailing perspective (of reality seen through art) all combine to lend credibility to the indictment, in a poem at once sombre and lucid.

Here Auden seems to go as far as poetry can in expressing his main preoccupation, 'the baffle of being'. Beyond, he is aware of something intuitable but unsayable – something that romantics and symbolists nevertheless try for, at their peril. Auden is wise enough not to attempt to reach what cannot be grasped, but like Shakespeare, peering into the mists beyond the border he can very occasionally give a sense of its presence:

> All the rest is silence
> On the other side of the wall;
> And the silence ripeness,
> And the ripeness all.

(*Selected Poems*, p. 128. *Collected Poems*, p. 311)

Beyond peace and war, politics, religion, philosophy, and psychology, all Auden's major concerns, lies what Joyce called 'the incertitude of the void'. An appropriate place to stop.

Part Three
Reference Section

Gazetteer

Auden maintained, and rightly, that he changed with time not with place. He is in no sense a topographical poet; if he starts with a particular place in mind when beginning a poem it is its significance he tries to capture not its identity. His woods, lakes or mountains are not any particular ones; they are representative ones. Similarly his cities are not those where he lived, Birmingham, London, New York; they are essential cities, symbols of industrialism or artificiality in contrast to rural society, or of civic responsibility as against the 'islands' of the private life, and so on. This brief gazetteer, then, has only minimal relevance to the appreciation of his work. It may, however, serve to bring into focus minor points of relevance scattered in the body of the book.

Berlin

Capital of pre-war Germany, where Auden discovered, and was influenced by political cabaret and expressionist drama.

Birmingham

Relevant in so far as it was there that Auden first made acquaintance with the big industrial city, but more importantly it was a base to explore the Yorkshire dales. That lovely limestone landscape of moderate mountains, fertile valleys, woods and waters provided a setting for a number of poems – and had the advantage of being easily assimilated into Italian and Grecian landscapes. Auden, however, was at least as interested in its old lead-mines and other abandoned workings.

Ischia

A picturesque island in the bay of Naples, with a colourful history. Auden rented a house there for the spring and summer of the years 1949 to 1957. 'Ischia' (*Collected Poems*, p. 416) is as near to a poem of place as Auden ever got. There he contrasts the island with 'soiled productive cities'. Epomeneo is the highest mountain (an extinct volcano), Restitua, the island's patron saint.

Kirchstetten

A village in Lower Austria, where Auden bought and converted a farmhouse (with the proceeds of an Italian literary prize) in 1958. It is celebrated in the poems of his book *About the House*. In 'Thanksgiving for a Habitat' (*Collected Poems*, p. 519) he gives thanks for having at last a real home, something between a planner's pen for a rational animal and upperclass ostentatious spaciousness, set in an organic community. He spent every spring and summer there until his death.

London

Mainly important, it seems, as the place where he spent six months with the G.P.O. film unit – an experience that gave him practice in writing for a more general public, and encouraged certain techniques – of 'shots' and 'scenes' – already to be found in his work.

New York

A dangerous, unfriendly city that strangely suited Auden. Here, freed from any obligation to be a leader of the Left, he could simply be a writer. In some degree it seems to have acted as a soul-purging place of penitence – but alienation rather suited Auden, and anyway America provided a bigger and better market for a lone intellectual (and a poet to boot) than did England.

Oxford

As an undergraduate there Auden first met other writers of a like mind, and emerged as a sort of student guru. He alleged that the most beautiful walk in that ancient city was along the canal by the gasworks and the municipal rubbish dump. When he returned as Professor of Poetry, however, his preferences seem to have been more orthodox. He has one poem on it ('Oxford', *Collected Poems*, p. 124). Otherwise it seems to have had no particular effect on his work.

Short Biographies

AUDEN, CONSTANCE ROSALIE (née Bicknell) Born 1875, daughter of the Rev. R. H. Bicknell, Vicar of Wroxham, Norfolk. Graduated in French at London University, but took up nursing with the idea of joining a Protestant medical mission in Africa. High Church, highly reiligious, and musical. Died August 1941.

AUDEN, GEORGE Born Repton, Derbyshire, 1872. Educated at Repton and Christ's College Cambridge, where he took Natural Sciences. Became an intern at St Bartholomew's Hospital, London, where he met Constance, who became his wife in 1899. Set up as general practitioner in York, where W. H. Auden, their third son was born, but moved to Birmingham to take up the posts of School Medical Officer and Professor of Public Health. Died 1957.

BRECHT, BERTOLT Born in Augsburg, Germany, 1898. A great admirer of Wedekind, the founder of German political cabaret, he wrote many poems in that style, as well as the 'alienating' political expressionist plays for which he is better known. Both almost certainly influenced Auden. Brecht remained a communist to the end of his life (Berlin 1956).

BRITTEN, BENJAMIN Born in Lowestoft, 1913. Educated at Gresham's School, Holt, and the Royal College of Music. One of the most eminent of British composers. He worked for the G.P.O. film unit from 1935–7, writing the music for 'Night Mail', which Auden set to words. He also collaborated with Auden on the operetta *Paul Bunyan*, set 'Our Hunting Fathers' to music, and also 'On this Island'. He became a Peer not long before his death in 1976.

EMPSON, WILLIAM Born in Yokefleet, East Yorkshire, 27 September 1906, almost an exact contemporary of Auden's. Educated at Winchester College, Hampshire, and Magdalene College, Cambridge. After performing brilliantly in both English and Maths as an undergraduate – and writing several plays, an epoch-making work of criticism, and an important book of poems – he did some postgraduate research, and then left England in 1931 to teach at the Tokyo National University till 1934. He taught at the National University, Peking, 1937–39 and again from 1947–52. During the war he was Chinese Editor of the Far-Eastern Section of the B.B.C. He also taught in the

157

U.S.A., and was Professor of English Literature at Sheffield University from 1953 to 1971 when he retired. Like Auden, in the Thirties. Empson had communist sympathies, but was sceptical about Auden and his associates – witness his well-known poem 'Just a Smack at Auden'. Like Auden, however, he believed that ideas had a place in poetry, and he came to admire the later Auden. But Empson's own poetry is more complex than Auden's, and its difficulties are different in kind and degree. He is perhaps most notable for several very different but equally important books of criticism.

FREUD, SIGMUND Born 1856. Professor of Neurology, Vienna University. Starting with hypnosis as a form of treatment for neurotic and psychotic states, he went on to develop his vastly important technique of psychoanalysis, becoming the most famous and influential of all psychologists. He discovered that ideas can produce physical symptoms, drew attention to the phenomenon of infant sexuality, to the immense importance of subconscious drives (especially that of sex), to the therapeutic significance of dreams, and the possibility of a death-wish underlying the pleasure-principle that seems to be basic. His is by far the greatest and longest-lasting influence on Auden. He died in England in 1939.

GASCOYNE, DAVID Born in Harrow, 1916; educated at Salisbury Cathedral Choir School and at the Regent Street Polytechnic. His first book of poems was published when he was sixteen; a novel followed in the next year. In 1935 he published the first English account of surrealism, followed next year by a volume of surrealist poems, *Man's Life is this Meat*. He lived in France during the Thirties (and again after the war), fought in the Spanish Civil War on the Republican side – for despite being a practising Catholic he was also a practising communist (as well as a surrealist). A position of triple conflict causing great mental stress, which is reflected in his verse. He represented the movement away from 'social' or 'public' poetry to interior – often private – neo-romantic poetry that characterised the later Thirties and the Forties. Dylan Thomas is the major representative of that school.

GRODDECK, GEORG Born at Bad Kösen, Germany, in 1866. A prolific writer, sharing some of Freud's ideas. Freud's Id seems derived from Groddeck's It. His views on psychosomatic disease, however, are more extreme than Freud's – but are expressed with a self-mockery and burlesque (similar to Kierkegaard's) that must have appealed to Auden: *v. The Unknown Self; a new approach to the problems of life, with special reference to disease*, Daniel, London 1932. Died 1934.

ISHERWOOD, CHRISTOPHER Born at Disley, Cheshire, 1904. Educated at the same prep school as Auden, and at Repton School and Corpus

Christi College, Cambridge. Like Auden, he went to Germany, but stayed much longer (1929–33). His Thirties' novels, *Goodbye to Berlin* and *Mr Norris Changes Trains*, are the product of that stay. A close friend of Auden's, at that period, he collaborated with him on three expressionist plays, *The Dog Beneath the Skin* (1935), *The Ascent of F6* (1937), and *On the Frontier* (1938). He accompanied Auden on the trip to China and collaborated with him on the ensuing volume *Journey to a War* (1939), and he left England for America with Auden in 1939. Isherwood, however, took to pacifism and eastern mysticism rather than to Christianity, and preferred California to New York. There he studied with the Vedanta Society and wrote filmscripts as well as continuing to write novels. His autobiographical volume *Lions and Shadows* (1938) is amusing as well as being a valuable source-book for the period.

KALLMAN, CHESTER Born January 1921 in Brooklyn, New York. He met Auden in 1939, shortly after his arrival at New York, and lived with him for most of the rest of their lives. He collaborated with Auden on the libretti of several operas (v. Chronology), wrote one libretto of his own (for *Tuscan Players* by Carlos Chávez), two translations of standard opera libretti and a certain amount of poetry, 1951–71. He was an excellent cook. Died Athens, January 1975.

KIERKEGAARD, SÖREN Born in Copenhagen, Denmark, 1813. Graduated in theology in 1840 – the delay in obtaining a degree being in part due to a life of pleasure and idleness that contrasted strongly with the industrious bigotry of later years. His conversion to Christian – but anti-clerical – extremism took place in 1838. After publishing a work on Hans Andersen in that year, he made his name as a thinker with *Either-Or*, one of the foundation-stones of Christian existentialist philosophy – if work so unsystematic can be called by that name. His influence on Auden is second only to that of Freud (Marx coming third). His death occurred in 1855.

LANE, HOMER Born U.S.A., 1876. Labourer, teacher, superintendent of reform schools, before moving to London to become a crank psychologist mingling Freud, Jung, and religion. His belief that all disease of the body was really disguised disease of the soul, was passed on to Auden by one of his patients, 'Loopy' Layard, whom he met in Berlin. Died 1925.

LEWIS, CECIL DAY Born of Anglo-Irish parents in Ballintogher, Southern Ireland, in 1904. He was educated at Sherborne and Wadham College, Oxford. He edited *Oxford Poetry* with Auden in 1927, was a more convinced communist than Auden, and a Party member, but like Auden he reverted to Anglicanism after the war, and like Auden became Professor of Poetry at Oxford. He was awarded the Poet Laureateship in 1968 and a C.B.E. During the war he was employed at the Ministry of information. He attained some fame not only as a poet but (under the pseudonym of Nicholas Blake) as a writer of detective fiction. He also wrote children's books and works of criticism. He died in 1972.

MACNEICE, LOUIS Born in Belfast, 1907. Educated at Marlborough and Merton College, Oxford. Appointed Lecturer in Classics at the University of Birmingham in 1930, Lecturer in Greek at Bedford College, London in 1936. He visited Spain in that year, as Auden did in 1937, and accompanied Auden in his trip to Iceland. From 1941 to the date of his death (1963) he wrote and produced radio plays and features for the B.B.C. (mostly in the great days of the Third Programme). In the Thirties he was a contributor to *New Verse*, but unlike Auden, Spender, and Day Lewis was never committed to communism. Like them, he has written critical as well as creative works. Unlike them, he never changed his beliefs radically, perhaps because they were less extreme in the first place.

MANN, ERIKA Born in Munich, Germany, 1905, daughter of Thomas Mann; emigrated from Germany in 1933 (when the Nazis came to power) and founded in Switzerland the anti-Nazi cabaret 'Die Pfeffermülle' (The Pepper-mill). Married Auden in 1935, for a British passport, went to the U.S.A. in 1936, and finally settled in Kilchberg, near Zürich (where she died in 1969). She wrote several books of stories for children and edited the letters of Thomas Mann.

MARX, KARL Born at Trier in 1818, a German subject of Jewish extraction. In Paris from 1843–45, where he was converted to socialism by reading Proudhon, and where he first met Engels. Expelled from France, he came to London where he lived, and wrote, until his death in 1883. *The Communist Manifesto* (with Engels) was published in 1847, the first volume of *Capital* in 1873 (the remaining two volumes being published from his papers by Engels after Marx's death). His economic theories, however, play little part in Auden's poetry.

MOSLEY, SIR OSWALD Born 1896, educated at Winchester and Sandhurst. He sat as a Conservative, as an Independent, and as a Labour M.P., before founding the British Union of Fascists in 1932. It attracted a considerable membership and obtained financial support from big business, but never obtained a single parliamentary seat. Mosley, and a number of his henchmen, were interned during the war. An attempted comeback after the war came to nothing. He retired to France, where he died in 1980.

NIEBUHR, REINHOLD Born in the U.S.A. 1892. A conspicuous figure in modern American Protestantism. He obtained two degrees at Yale, and thereafter did much theological and political work on university campuses. He alleged the 'mild moralistic idealism' of much of American Christianity to be irrelevant, and advocated a more dogmatic ethics, stressing inherent human sinfulness and pride, especially in social affairs. He developed an Augustinian theology. *The Nature and Destiny of Man* (2 vols 1941–43) is said to have influenced Auden. Auden's brother says that his conversion to Christianity was due to the shock of their mother's death. Perhaps Niebuhr reinforced Auden's adherence to the Episcopalian Church, which assorts rather oddly with his existentialism. Niebuhr's assertion that the final answer to human problems lies beyond history, however, is not inconsistent with Kierkegaard's view on the matter.

SPENDER, STEPHEN Born in London, 1909, son of the writer Harold Spender. Educated at University College School, London, and University College, Oxford, where he was a contemporary of Auden and MacNeice. He edited *Oxford Poetry* in 1930, with MacNeice and Bernard Spender. Like Auden, Spender went to Germany for a prolonged stay after leaving Oxford, and later travelled widely in Europe with Isherwood. Like Auden, too, he was in Spain for a time during the Civil War and did propaganda work for the Republican side. His autobiographical book, *World Within World* (Hamish Hamilton 1951) gives a fascinating account of the complex situation there, and is a valuable companion volume to George Orwell's *Homage to Catalonia*.

The change in Spender's political opinions is reflected in the difference between *Forward from Liberalism* (Gollancz 1937), which argues for Marxism, and *Life and the Poet* (Secker 1942), which argues against it. Both his early Marxism and his present liberalism seem to spring from an intense sympathy with the downtrodden. Though greatly admiring, and influenced by, Auden he was never able to be so detached and unromantic, nor did he renounce humanism for religion when his political opinions changed. Like Auden, he has taught in many American universities and also in the University of London. His literary output in verse and prose is almost as prodigious as Auden's.

STRAVINSKY, IGOR Born 1882 at Oranienbaum, near St Petersburg, Russia. Studied under Rimsky-Korsakov, and composed for the Diaghilev ballet company. In 1940 he settled in America, where he met Auden, collaborating with him and Kallman on the opera *The Rake's Progress* (1951). He died in Venice in 1971.

THOMAS, DYLAN Born in Swansea, Wales, 1914. Educated at the local grammar school; then joined the *South Wales Evening Post* as a reporter.

During the war he worked for the B.B.C., his most famous work, *Under Milk Wood*, being written as a radio play for the Third Programme. His political views were not dissimilar to those of Auden in the Thirties. Indeed he took the opportunity (along with David Gascoyne) of expressing left-wing revolutionary sympathies while praising Auden in the Auden Double Number of *New Verse* (November 1937) – a number sealing Auden's status as the Grand Master of the period. In literary terms, however, he is almost as different as Gascoyne (q.v.). His poetry is personal, physical, emotive and semi-surreal, quite unlike Auden's. It seems to represent a pre-war feeling that the outer world has got to be so far out of control that the poet must turn inward, in despair, for his subject-matter. His death occurred in New York in 1953.

Bibliography

The following booklists include all the texts used in the present work, but also give a selection of other books for those who might wish to follow up one aspect or another. A complete list of books, articles and reviews by and about Auden is to be found in Gingerich (*v.* section 5. below). Auden's works – and many contemporary publications by other writers – are also to be found in the Bibliographical Chronology.

Place of publication: London, unless otherwise stated.

1 *Works by Auden*

POETRY

Colleted Poems (ed. E. Mendelson) Faber, 1976
The English Auden (ed. E. Mendelson) Faber, 1977
Selected Poems (ed. E. Mendelson) Faber, 1979

PROSE

Forewords and Afterwords (ed. E. Mendelson) Faber, 1973
The Dyer's Hand, (ed. E. Mendelson) Faber, 1963
Selected Essays (ed. E. Mendelson) Faber, 1964

2 *Biography*

AUDEN, W. H. 'Letter to Lord Byron' *The English Auden* (*v.* above)
ISHERWOOD, C. *Lions and Shadows*, Hogarth, 1937
OSBORNE, C. *W. H. Auden: The Life of a Poet*, Eyre Methuen, 1980
SPENDER, S. (ed.) *W. H. Auden: A tribute*, Weidenfeld and Nicolson, 1974
STRAVINSKY, IGOR, and Robert Craft. *Themes and Episodes*, New York, Knopf, 1966.

3 *Cultural and historical background*

AIKEN, H. D. (ed.) *The Age of Ideology*, Frederick Muller, 1956
(Chapters on the philosophy of Marx and Kierkegaard)
BERGONZI, B. *Reading the Thirties*, Macmillan, 1979
CALVOCORESSI, P. *World Politics since 1945*, Longman, 1977

CAUTE, D. *Essential Writings of Karl Marx*, Panther Books, 1967

COLE, G. D. H. *What Marx Really Meant*, Gollancz, 1934

CONRAD, P. *Imagining America*, Routledge and Kegan Paul, 1980

FAIRCHILD, F. N. *Religious Trends in English Poetry*, Vol. 6, New York, Columbia University Press, 1968

FISCHER, E. (ed.) *Marx in His Own Words*, Penguin, 1970

FRASER, G. S. *The Modern Writer and His World*, Andre Deutsch, 1955

FREUD, S. *Beyond the Pleasure Principle*, Hogarth, 1922

    The Interpretation of Dreams, Allen and Unwin, 1913

    The Psychopathology of Everyday Life, Benn, 1930

GRODDECK, G. *The Book of the It*, New York, Nervous and Mental Disease Publishing Co., 1928.

    The Unknown Self, Daniel, 1932

HUXLEY, A. *Eyeless in Gaza*, Chatto and Windus, 1936

    Ends and Means, Chatto and Windus, 1937

    (Important and lucid expositions of pacifist theory)

KAUFMAN, W. (ed.) *Existentialism*, Thames & Hudson, 1956

KIERKEGAARD, S. *Kierkegaard*, ed. and introduced by Auden, Cassell and Co. 1955

    Fear and Trembling and The Sickness Unto Death, (trans. W. Lowrie), New York, Doubleday Anchor Books, 1954

LEHMANN, J. (ed.) *New Writing*, Hogarth, 1936–39

LEWIS, CECIL DAY. *The Buried Day*, Chatto and Windus, 1960

LEWIS, WYNDHAM. *Revenge for Love*, Methuen, 1937

    (A rare, and excellent, anti-communist novel, highlighting the polarities of the period)

MACNEICE, LOUIS. *The Strings Are False: An Unfinished Autobiography*. Oxford University Press, 1966.

MARX, KARL. *Capital*, New York, Modern Library Giant, 1940–?

    Marx in His Own Words (*v.* Fischer, ed.)

MILIBAND, R. *Marxism and Politics*, O.U.P., 1977.

NIEBUHR, R. *Moral Man and Immoral Society*, New York, Scribner's, 1932

    The Nature and Destiny of Man (2 vols), New York, Scribner's, 1941–3

ORWELL, G. *Down and Out in Paris and London*, Gollancz, 1933

    Homage to Catalonia, Secker and Warburg, 1938

    The Road to Wigan Pier, Gollancz, 1937

    Collected Essays, Journalism and Letters, Penguin, 1970

ROBERTS, M. (ed.) *New Country*, Hogarth, 1933

    New Signatures, Hogarth, 1932

RODWAY, A. (ed.) *Poetry of the Thirties*, Longman, 1967

SCULLY, J. (ed.) *Modern Poets on Modern Poetry*, Fontana, 1970

SPENDER, S. *The Creative Element*, Hamish Hamilton, 1953

    The Destructive Element, Cape, 1935

    Forward from Liberalism, Gollancz, 1937

    Life and the Poet, Secker and Warburg, 1942

    The Thirties and After, Fontana, 1978

World Within World, Hamish Hamilton, 1951
SYMONS, J. *The Thirties*, Cresset Press, 1960
TAYLOR, A. J. P. *English History 1914–45*, Penguin, 1970
WILLIAMS, R. *Culture and Society 1780–1950*, Penguin, 1961

4 *Criticism*

BEACH, J. W. *The Making of the Auden Canon*, Minneapolis, University of Minnesota Press, 1957
BLAIR, J. G. *The Poetic Art of W. H. Auden*, Princeton, University Press, 1965
BUELL, F. *W. H. Auden as a Social Poet*, Ithaca and London, Cornell University Press, 1973
CARTER, R. 'W. H. Auden, City Without Walls', *Agenda*, Summer 1978
COOK, F. W. 'The Wise Fool: W. H. Auden and the Management' *Twentieth Century*, September 1960
DAVISON, D. *W. H. Auden*, Evans Bros., 1970
DUCHENE, F. *The Case of the Helmeted Airman: A Study of W. H. Auden's Poetry*. Chatto & Windus, 1972
FULLER, J. *A Reader's Guide to W. H. Auden*, Thames and Hudson, 1970
GRIGSON, G. (ed.) Auden Double Number of *New Verse*, November 1937
HOGGART, R. *Auden: An Introductory Essay*, Chatto & Windus, 1951
W. H. Auden, Longman, 1957
HYNES, S. *The Auden Generation*, Bodley Head, 1976
JOHNSON, R. *Man's Place: An Essay on Auden*, New York, Cornell University Press, 1973
MAXWELL, D. E. S. *Poets of the Thirties*, Routledge & Kegan Paul, 1969
REPLOGLE, J. *Auden's Poetry*, Methuen, 1969
RODWAY, A. 'Logicless Grammar in Audenland', *London Magazine*, March 1965
SPEARS, M. (ed.) *Auden*, New Jersey, Prentice-Hall Inc., 1964
The Poetry of W. H. Auden, Oxford University Press, 1963

5 *Bibliography*

BLOOMFIELD, B. C. & MENDELSON, E. *W. H. Auden: A Bibliography 1942–69*, Charlottesville, University Press of Virginia, 1972
GINGERICH, M. E. *W. H. Auden: A Reference Guide*, Boston, Mass., S. K. Hull and Co.; and London, George Prior, 1977

6 *Recommendations*

Choice, from a list already selective, is invidious. But for those with little time, and perhaps little inclination, to explore much further than this *Preface* to Auden, the following seem the most useful and enjoyable aids to an extended appreciation of his poetry:

TEXTS : *Selected Poems*, ed. Mendelson
BIOGRAPHY : *Lions and Shadows*, Isherwood.
CULTURAL AND HISTORICAL BACKGROUND: *Marx in His Own Words* ed. Fischer; *The Interpretation of Dreams*, Freud; *Kierkegaard*, ed. Auden; *The Thirties and After*, Spender; *English History 1914–45*, Taylor
CRITICISM : *Auden's Poetry*, Replogle.

General Index

Index to Auden's poetry and prose

Acknowledgements

A special debt of gratitude is owed to my colleague Dr Ron Carter for his assistance and encouragement, and for his kindness in reading the manuscript through. Special thanks are also due to Faber and Faber for permitting the large amount of quotation necessary for a work, and author, of this kind. Thanks are also due to Weidenfeld & Nicolson for permission to quote from *W. H. Auden: A Tribute*, and for illustrations from the same work; to Eyre Methuen for illustrations from *W. H. Auden: The Life of a Poet*, to Cornell University Press for permission to quote from *Auden as Social Poet*; to J. M. Dent & Sons for the quotation from *Deaths and Entrances*; to Routledge & Kegan Paul for the quotation from *Imagining America*, and to the Open University for the quotation from *Agenda*.

We are grateful to the following for permission to reproduce copyright material:

Faber & Faber Ltd for extracts from *The English Auden: Poems, Essays and Dramatic Writings 1927–39* edited by E. Mendelson (1977); Faber & Faber Ltd and Random House Inc. for extracts from *Collected Poems* by W. H. Auden edited by E. Mendelson (1976), *Forewords and Afterwords* by W. H. Auden edited by E. Mendelson (1973), *Readings from Selected Essays* by W. H. Auden (1964), *Selected Poems* by W. H. Auden edited by E. Mendelson (1979) and *The Dyer's Hand and Other Essays* by W. H. Auden (1963); George Weidenfeld and Nicolson Ltd for extracts from *W. H. Auden: A Tribute* edited by Stephen Spender.

We are grateful to the following for permission to reproduce photographs:

Britten-Pears Library, Aldeburgh, page 28; Professor Edward Callan, Western Michigan University, page 33 (photo Luigi Coppa); Daily Telegraph Colour Library, page 142 (photo Horst Munzig); GPO, page 104; Mark Gerson, pages 64 and 151; Lockwood Memorial Library, Buffalo, New York, page 89; Giorgio de Chirico, *Gare Montparnasse (The Melancholy of Departure)*, 1914, Museum of Modern Art, New York, page 115; National Portrait Gallery, page 40; New York Times, page 141; Oxfordshire County Libraries, pages 21 and 23; Billett Potter, Oxford, page 129; Sotheby's, Belgravia, page 54 (photo Cecil Beaton); Weidenfeld and Nicolson Archives, pages ii, 19

(John Auden), 29 (photo Stephen Spender) and 42 (photo Natasha Spender).

The painting *Broadway Boogie-Woogie* by Piet Mondrian, 1942–3 (oil on canvas, 127 × 127 cm) is reproduced on the cover by permission of the Museum of Modern Art, New York.